"Wow! I have never found learning so easy and fascinating. I believe this volume will be invaluable to any student who is interested in taking considerably less time to study, fascinating to trivia buffs, and engrossing to the lay public who might never expect to encounter in one book the nuts and bolts of so many different walks of life. This is a keeper."

—Joe Edley, Three-Time U.S. National
Scrabble Champion (1980, 1992, 2000)

"While Rod Evans's book will be valuable to introductory students in numerous disciplines, it will be *particularly* valuable as a model for inventing one's own mnemonics."

—Joel Wapnick, 1999 World Scrabble Champion,
1998 Canadian National Scrabble Champion,
1983 U.S. National Scrabble Champion

"Instructive and entertaining!"

—Edwin Newman, longtime NBC News correspondent,
author of *Strictly Speaking* and *A Civil Tongue*

"If there's a mnemonic device Rod Evans has missed, good luck finding it. There are more than a few in *Every Good Boy Deserves Fudge* that I'll be using next time *Jeopardy!* comes calling."

—Brad Rutter, winner of *Jeopardy!* 2001 Tournament of Champions,
the Million Dollar Masters Tournament,
and the Ultimate Tournament of Champions

THE BOOK OF MNEMONIC DEVICES

EVERY GOOD BOY DESERVES FUDGE

Rod L. Evans, Ph.D.

A PERIGEE BOOK

A PERIGEE BOOK
Published by the Penguin Group
Penguin Group (USA) Inc.
375 Hudson Street, New York, New York 10014, USA
Penguin Group (Canada), 90 Eglinton Avenue East, Suite 700, Toronto, Ontario M4P 2Y3, Canada
(a division of Pearson Penguin Canada Inc.)
Penguin Books Ltd., 80 Strand, London WC2R 0RL, England
Penguin Group Ireland, 25 St. Stephen's Green, Dublin 2, Ireland (a division of Penguin Books Ltd.)
Penguin Group (Australia), 250 Camberwell Road, Camberwell, Victoria 3124, Australia
(a division of Pearson Australia Group Pty. Ltd.)
Penguin Books India Pvt. Ltd., 11 Community Centre, Panchsheel Park, New Delhi—110 017, India
Penguin Group (NZ), 67 Apollo Drive, Rosedale, North Shore 0745, Auckland, New Zealand
(a division of Person New Zealand Ltd.)
Penguin Books (South Africa) (Pty.) Ltd., 24 Sturdee Avenue, Rosebank, Johannesburg 2196,
South Africa

Penguin Books Ltd., Registered Offices: 80 Strand, London WC2R 0RL, England

While the author has made every effort to provide accurate telephone numbers and Internet
addresses at the time of publication, neither the publisher nor the author assumes any responsibility
for errors, or for changes that occur after publication. Further, the publisher does not have any control over and does not assume any responsibility for author or third-party websites or their content.

First edition: August 2007

Library of Congress Cataloging-in-Publication Data

Evans, Rod L., 1956–
    Every good boy deserves fudge : the book of mnemonic devices / Rod L. Evans.— 1st ed.
        p. cm.
    Includes bibliographical references.
    ISBN 978-0-399-53351-8
    1. Mnemonics. I. Title.
    BF385.E77 2007
    153.1'4—dc22

                                                                                    2007011894

PRINTED IN THE UNITED STATES OF AMERICA

10 9 8 7 6 5 4 3 2 1

Most Perigee books are available at special quantity discounts for bulk purchases for sales promo-
tions, premiums, fund-raising, or educational use. Special books, or book excerpts, can also be created to fit specific needs. For details, write: Special Markets, Penguin Group (USA) Inc., 375
Hudson Street, New York, New York 10014.

ACKNOWLEDGMENTS

My deep thanks go to my literary agents, Sheree Bykofsky and Janet Rosen; my editor at Perigee, Meg Leder; the managing editor at Perigee, Jennifer Eck; the copyeditor for this book, Candace Levy; my friends who helped edit the typescript, Justin Gruver, Abbott Saks, and the polymathic Curtis Brooks; and my good friend and extraordinary administrative assistant, Robin Hudgins. My thanks go also to Dr. David Robinson, *Mnemonics & More for Psychiatry*; Stan Cody, *Teaching Out of the Box*; Jim Sarris, *Comic Mnemonics: A Fun, Easy Way to Remember Spanish Verbs*; Bart Benne and Rowman & Littlefield, *Waspleg and Other Mnemonics*; Meish Goldish and Scholastic Inc., *Memory-Boosting Songs for Content Area Learning*; Geoff Kuenning; and Steve Brügge, Albuquerque's Eisenhower Middle School.

This book has been enriched by the hard work of many people. I am deeply grateful.

CONTENTS

INTRODUCTION
MNEMONICS

A mnemonic, or mnemonic device, is a technique or strategy for improving or strengthening memory. The word *mnemonic* comes from "Mnemosyne," the name of one of the Titans in Greek mythology. The Titans were a race of giants who warred against the gods. Mnemosyne, whose name relates to the Greek *mnēmonikos* (mindful), was courted by Zeus, the king of the gods. She bore him nine daughters, the Muses, four of whom were Muses of poetry. Before writing was invented, poets needed prodigious memories. Zeus was attracted to Mnemosyne when he wanted a way to record the triumphs of the gods. Together Zeus and Mnemosyne produced the nine Muses, whose specialties (music, poetry of different kinds, history, and astronomy) inspire mnemonics today.

Although some people scoff at mnemonics, these devices have proved extremely effective in helping people remember not only historic dates, spelling, and geography but also science, law, and medicine—and numerous other fields. Mnemonic devices are almost as old as Mnemosyne herself. Legend has it that the Greek poet Simonides was an early mnemonist who was able to visualize where guests were sitting at a party he had attended. That ability came in handy because after he left one such gathering, the roof of the building fell in, requiring someone to identify the crushed bodies.

Roman mnemonists were able to remember their speeches by associating various points in their talks with familiar pieces of furniture in their homes or familiar buildings on some streets. As they delivered their speeches, they imagined these rooms, buildings, or streets and were able to remember the ideas they had associated with each item.

In the Middle Ages, when illiteracy was widespread, people used visual symbols to embody object lessons. Accordingly, the seven deadly sins were represented by a lion (pride), a serpent (envy), a bear (sloth), a fox (greed), a swine (gluttony), a unicorn (anger), and a scorpion (lust). Today's mnemonics—which emphasize rhymes, acrostics ("Every good boy deserves fudge"), and acronyms (HOMES for the Great Lakes)—came into prominence especially when English schoolboys had to memorize a host of things, including the kings of England and Latin grammar.

The idea behind mnemonic devices is simple: to connect what is unfamiliar to what is familiar. For example, the word *mnemonic* itself can be recalled by thinking of a memorable sentence, say, "**M**om **n**eeds **e**asy **m**ethods **o**f **n**oting **i**mportant **c**ontent." Note that the first letter of each word, when put together, forms the word *mnemonic*. Generations of students have learned the Great Lakes by recalling HOMES, an acronym for Huron, Ontario, Michigan, Erie, and Superior. Once people are familiar with the names of the Great Lakes, they can use mnemonic devices to recall the lakes in order of descending surface area: "**S**am's **h**orse **m**ust **e**at **o**ats." It's a great deal easier to recall that sentence than to remember the names of the lakes in a particular sequence—Superior, Huron, Michigan, Erie, and Ontario—without a mnemonic device.

HOW TO CREATE EFFECTIVE MNEMONICS

Often the sillier and more ridiculous the mnemonic device, the better. Anatomy students who need to know the branches of the facial nerve will find the sentence "**T**eddy **Z**ucker's **b**owels move constantly" a great deal easier to remember than the individual terms *temporal*, *zygomatic*, *buccal*, *mandibular*, and *cervical*. An effective but less gross mnemonic could be "Ten zebras bought my car."

Similarly, consider these sentences:

- Camels often sit down carefully.
- Perhaps their joints creak.
- Possibly early oiling might prevent permanent rheumatism.

Such ridiculous sentences have helped countless students recall the following geological time periods: Cambrian, Ordovician, Silurian, Devonian, Carboniferous, Permian, Triassic, Jurassic, Cretaceous, Paleocene, Eocene, Oligocene, Miocene, Pliocene, Pleistocene, and Recent.

THE MOST POPULAR MNEMONICS

Most mnemonics today fall into one of four classes: acrostic sentences, acronyms, rhymes, or wordplay. Acrostic mnemonics are sentences in which the first letter of each word is the first letter of one of the things you need to remember. Acrostics are best when they are funny, ridiculous, or gross. Those that are funny and that describe something easy to visualize are ideal, as when one visualizes the earlier-mentioned arthritic camels or Teddy Zucker, the guy with the overactive bowels. Acrostics are especially useful for long lists of things whose names don't begin with vowels. A famous acrostic for the planets Mercury, Venus, Earth, Mars, Jupiter, Saturn, Uranus, Neptune, and Pluto is "My very energetic mother just served us nine pizzas," which can be replaced by "My very evil mother just served us newts," should you agree with the 2006 reclassification of Pluto as a dwarf planet rather than a full-fledged one.

When the lists or terms to be recalled are shorter and have some vowels, acronyms can be useful. An acronym is a word created by using the first letter of each word of the information to be recalled. Some common acronyms are NATO (North Atlantic Treaty Organization), RAM (random access memory), and scuba (self-contained underwater breathing apparatus).

Acronyms are also useful when the order of the items to be remembered is unimportant—for example, HOMES for the Great Lakes.

In recalling which four words of the first declension are masculine, Latin students learn the acronym PAIN, standing for *poeta* (poet), *agricola* (farmer), *incola* (inhabitant), and *nauta* (sailor). Similarly, math students recall the order of operations when solving a math problem by the acronymn PEMDAS: **P**eople should **p**erform operations within **p**arentheses first, then **e**xponents, then solve **m**ultiplication and **d**ivision from left to right, and finally solve **a**ddition and **s**ubtraction from left to right.

Rhyming mnemonics are useful for remembering wise sayings, spellings of tricky words, historic dates, and rules of thumb. Who hasn't learned the most famous spelling rule?

> *I* before *E*
> Except after *C*,
> Or in rhyming with *A*,
> As in *neighbor* or *weigh*.

Author Murray Suid, in his excellent *Demonic Mnemonics*, explains that we can remember how to spell *oboe* if we ask, "Can you play an oboe with your toe?" That mnemonic device uses a rhyme and wordplay.

Although most of the mnemonic devices in this book fall into one of the four classes just described, there are some that don't fit neatly into one of these groups. Mnemonics you have made up yourself are often the most useful. Consider the following mnemonic, which I created for remembering the number of bones in the adult human body: **Hbo**nes = **6**. For me, the equation signifies 206 (the number of bones in the body). The *H* represents "human," the *b* represents "2" because it is the second letter of the mnemonic device and the second letter of our alphabet, the *o* represents "zero," and the *6* represents the number of letters in the device and the last digit of 206.

OTHER MNEMONIC TECHNIQUES

Chaining

Chaining is a way to link facts by making associations between them. Chaining can involve visualizing a series of connected images or developing a story to connect terms or concepts. Suppose, for example, you want to recall a grocery list consisting of eggs, milk, bread, laundry detergent, and orange juice. You could imagine or visualize a huge egg, which cracks open, revealing a milk carton, which breaks open, revealing a jug of laundry detergent, which you open and find orange juice. By connecting a series of strange or ridiculous mental images, you can recall long lists.

The idea behind chaining can be compared to wordplay, as when you ask, "**What** thief could steal a **jewel** every **second**?" That question, asked by authors Russell Kahn and Tom Meltzer in *How to Remember Everything, Grades 9–12,* can help people recall the definition of a *watt*, a unit of power. One watt is equal to one joule per second.

Chunking

Chunking involves making information more manageable by grouping related information into smaller, more manageable units. Telephone numbers are easier to remember in their chunks (202-555-7337) than as a long string (2025557337).

The principle of chunking is useful for not only numbers but also any facts classifiable into distinct groups. Chunking is useful for recalling the parts of the ear. You could, for example, recall the parts involving the canals—auditory canal and semicircular canal; then the parts named after tools or instruments—hammer, anvil, stirrup, and eardrum; and finally the parts located at the back of the inner ear—cochlea and auditory nerve. If you want to improve your vocabulary, use chunking. For example, learn synonyms in clusters (*talkative, garrulous, loquacious*) or recall words that share the same root (*culprit, exculpate, inculpate*).

Keywords

A keyword is a familiar word that sounds like the word or information you need to remember. If you meet someone named Bill, you conjure a mental image of him eating a utility bill. If you meet a guy named Frank, you can picture his head turning into a frankfurter. Similarly, a person named Robin can be pictured as a bird.

The Loci Method

The loci method is one of the oldest known mnemonic techniques. The word *loci* means "places," and the loci method associates familiar places with information. You might have used the loci method to find something you've misplaced. Suppose, for example, English class has just ended, and you realize that your keys are missing. You might be able to find your keys by retracing all the places you were that day. Before you were in the English class, you had math in another building. You then go to the math class, but see no keys along the way or in the room. Then you recall that you were in French class before math, so you retrace your steps to French class. The keys, though, are not found. Now you recall that you had bought some milk at a convenience store right before French class. When you go to the convenience store, the cashier recognizes you as the person who left keys on the counter.

In *How to Remember Everything, Grades 6–8*, Ellen Gibson and Nick Guastaferro explain how you can learn the different properties of waves by using the loci method. The crest of a wave, its highest point, can be associated with the ceiling of your bedroom if you write the word *crest* on an index card and then tape it on the ceiling. To associate the trough of a wave, its lowest point, with the floor of your bedroom, tape an index card with the word *trough* to the floor. The wavelength, the distance between successive crests or troughs, can be associated with a ruler (known for measuring distances) by placing a card with the word *wavelength* by the ruler. Frequency, the number of wavelengths occurring in a given unit of time, can be associated with a calendar, which represents time, by placing a card with the word *frequency* by a calendar. Finally, amplitude, the height of a wave, or the distance from the rest position of the wave to the crest or trough, can be associated with your bed (where you rest) by placing a card with the word *amplitude* on your bed.

Although the loci technique doesn't require taping index cards to physical objects, placing such cards with bright-colored words in different places could help you remember a series of interrelated things. As noted earlier, the loci method was popular in ancient times, when Greek or Roman politicians used it to recall points to be made in speeches.

Pegwords

A mnemonic technique for recalling such things as long lists or large numbers is the pegword method. A pegword is a short word that describes an easy-to-visualize object whose name rhymes with a specific number. Although you can develop your own pegword list, the following pegwords are commonly used to represent the first six numbers: *bun* (for one), *shoe* (for two), *tree* (for three), *door* (for four), *hive* (for five), and *sticks* (for six).

A pegword mnemonic can help you remember things in the correct order. To recall the number 23, you can visualize shoes growing on a tree, since the word *shoe* can represent "two" and *tree* can represent "three." Suppose you want first to stop at the post office to mail a letter, next buy a cup of coffee, and then buy some gasoline. You could picture the following images: You visualize opening a bun (peg one) and finding dozens of envelopes, which then fall on top of your shoes (peg two), on which you now spill hot coffee. The hot coffee soaking your shoes causes you angrily to kick a tree (peg three), out of which flows gasoline. The pegs enable you to link a bun, shoe, and tree with the post office, coffee, and gasoline, respectively.

When linking the images, try to visualize action because moving images will usually be more memorable than stationary ones. Furthermore, for some people ridiculous images, or at least images that are in certain respects extraordinary, are especially helpful.

The more familiar you become with mnemonic devices, the more easily you'll remember lots of information and the more easily you'll be able to create your own mnemonic devices.

I hope that you'll enjoy these mnemonics as much as I've enjoyed presenting them. Good luck!

ASTRONOMY

- -

The Planets of Our Solar System (before 2006, when Pluto was officially reclassified as a "dwarf planet")

- My very educated mother just showed us nine planets.
- My very easy mnemonic just summed up nine planets.
- My very energetic mother just served us nine pizzas.

Mercury	Saturn
Venus	Uranus
Earth	Neptune
Mars	Pluto
Jupiter	

Note: Although the planets are usually in the order indicated by the mnemonic devices listed, for 20 out of every 248 years, Pluto is closer to the Sun than Neptune (as from 1979 to 1999). For those years, use the following mnemonic: My very evil mother just sold us poisonous nightshade.

The Planets of Our Solar System (after the 2006 reclassification of Pluto)

- My very eccentric mother just served us nude.
- My very evil mother just served us nothing.
- My very eccentric mailman just showed up naked.
- Many very eccentric men just specified unwanted nomenclature.

Mercury	Jupiter
Venus	Saturn
Earth	Uranus
Mars	Neptune

The Four Largest Planets (in Order of Decreasing Size)

- **J-SUN**

Jupiter   Uranus
Saturn   Neptune

The 10 Largest Bodies in the Solar System (in Order of Decreasing Size)

- **S**unny **J-SUN** **e**ventually **v**isited **M**ars **g**ratefully **t**oday.

Sun   Earth
Jupiter   Venus
Saturn   Mars
Uranus   Ganymede
Neptune   Titan

Note: Ganymede is the largest moon of Jupiter and of the solar system. Titan is the largest moon of Saturn.

The Planets (Largest to Smallest; before 2006)

- **J-SUN** **e**mptied **V**anessa's **M&M** **p**late.

Jupiter   Venus
Saturn   Mars
Uranus   Mercury
Neptune   Pluto
Earth

The Planets (Smallest to Largest; before 2006)

- **P**layful **m**en **m**arry **VENUS** **j**ubilantly.

Pluto   Neptune
Mercury   Uranus
Mars   Saturn
Venus   Jupiter
Earth

The Mean Distance of Each Planet to the Sun (in Astronomical Units)

One astronomical unit is the mean distance of the Earth to the Sun, about 93 million miles. In the following scale, $1.00 equals 1 astronomical unit, or 93 million miles.[1]

Mercury	$0.39
Venus	$0.72
Earth	$1.00
Mars	$1.50
Jupiter	$5.20
Saturn	$9.50
Uranus	$19.00
Neptune	$30.00
Pluto	$39.50

Note: Pluto is usually about 39.5 units farther from the Sun than the Earth is.

Neptune's Named Moons

- Neptune told Diana good looks predict troubling nemeses.

Naiad	Larissa
Thalassa	Proteus
Despina	Triton
Galatea	Nereid

The Two Planets with no Moons

- MerVe

Mercury
Venus

The Moons of Mars

- **P**retty **d**inky

  Phobos
  Deimos

The Galilean Moons of Jupiter

- **I**ce grows **e**ven **c**older.

  Io   Europa
  Ganymede   Callisto

The Waxing and Waning of the Moon

- **DOC**
- **COD**

  D=waxing moon
  O=full moon
  C=waning moon

  DOC represents the phases in the Northern Hemisphere, and COD represents the phases in the Southern Hemisphere.

- **L**eft-hand curve **d**ecreasing
- **R**ight-hand curve **i**ncreasing

- O Lady Moon, your horns point toward the east;
  Shine, be increased;
  O Lady Moon, your horns point toward the west;
  Wane, be at rest.[2]

The Five Brightest Stars (in Descending Order)

▪ Some constellations actually aid voyagers.

Sirius	Arctus
Canopus	Vega
Alpha Centauri	

Note: Alpha Centauri is visible in only the Southern Hemisphere.

The Five Closest Stars to Earth (Farthest to Closest)

▪ Astronomers bless wisely locating stars.

Alpha Centauri	Lalande
Barnard's Star	Sirius
Wolf	

Note: Sirius is the closest star visible to the naked eye.

Spectral Classification of Stars (Hottest to Coolest)

▪ Oh, be a fine girl/guy, kiss me right now, sweetheart!

O	K
B	M
A	R
F	N
G	S

Note: Stars can also be classified as L-type or T-type when they are so small that they don't generate enough heat to begin nuclear fusion.

AVIATION

First Successful Wright Brothers' Flight

- The Wright Brothers had glee in 1903.

Checklist for Takeoffs

- **CIGAR**

  controls   altitude indicator
  instruments   radio
  gas

How to Determine a Compass Heading

- **T**he **v**armints **m**ake **d**evilish **c**ompany.

  true heading ± variation = magnetic heading ±
     deviation = compass heading

The Federal Aviation Regulations Concerning Drinking Alcohol

- Eight hours from the bottle to the throttle.

How to Tell the Direction the Compass Will Swing When Air Speed Changes

- **ANDS**

  accelerate north
  decelerate south

Adjustment for Magnetic North

Because the magnetic North Pole isn't the same as the true North Pole, pilots must adjust for compass variation relative to the line of zero magnetic variation.

- East is least.
  West is best.

  east = subtract
  west = add

  Note: The same tactic is used for determining flying altitude. Pilots flying east fly at odd altitudes (such as 33,000 feet), whereas those flying west fly at even altitudes (such as 34,000 feet).

The Four Cs for Emergencies in Flight

- Confess the predicament to a ground radio station.
- Communicate with the ground radio link.
- Climb in altitude, if possible, for better radar and direction finding.
- Comply with the advice and instructions received.

Potential Evacuation of a Commercial Flight

To help crew members recall what to say to the captain

- **TEST**

  type of emergency (equipment malfunction, fire, terrorism)
  evacuation (yes or no)
  signal to be given by the captain (oral, alarm, lights)
  time (number of minutes till evacuation)

Checklist for Documents Required in the Cockpit

- **ARROW**

  air-worthiness certificate
  registration
  radio permit

  owner's manual
  weight and balance control
  form

Note: The weight and balance control form describes the airplane's center of gravity.

Checklist for Landings

- **GUMPS**

  gas
  undercarriage
  mixture

  pilot strapped in
  speed

When to Administer Oxygen to a Passenger

- **IN USA**

  irrational behavior
  note from passenger's doctor
  unconscious but breathing
  severe chest pain
  asthma attack

U.S. Manned Space Programs (Chronological Order)

- **M**any **g**reat **a**stronauts **s**kygaze.

  Mercury
  Gemini

  Apollo
  Skylab

BASEBALL

Baseball's First Hall of Fame Inductees

- Writers can rate male jocks.

Wagner, Honus	Mathewson, Christy
Cobb, Ty	Johnson, Walter
Ruth, Babe	

The Eight Players Involved in the Chicago "Black" Sox Scandal of 1919[3]

- Chicago White's Joe foolishly gambled with mobster Rothstein.

PLAYER	POSITION	CAREER STATISTICS
Cicotte, Eddie	pitcher	ERA 2.38
Williams, Lefty	pitcher	ERA 3.13
Jackson, Joe	left field	BA .356
Felsch, Oscar "Happy"	center field	BA .293
Gandil, Chick	first base	BA .277
Weaver, Buck	third base	BA .272
McMullin, Fred	utility infield	BA .256
Risberg, Swede	shortstop	BA .243

Note: During the 1919 World Series, the Chicago White Sox purposely lost to the Cincinnati Reds. The mnemonic sentence describes the event. "Shoeless" Joe Jackson, Chicago's heavy-hitting left fielder, received a bribe of $5,000 to throw the series. Arnold Rothstein was the New York gambler who financed and possibly orchestrated the fixing of the series by bribing Jackson and the other players. Although Buck Weaver refused to participate in the fix, he was later banned for not having reported it.

The End of Joe DiMaggio's 56-Game Hitting Streak[4]

- Ken Keltner killed it in Cleveland.

Note: Keltner ended the streak on July 17, 1941.

Baseball's Last .400 Hitter[5]

- .41 in '41

Note: Ted Williams hit .406 (which rounds off to 41%) for the Boston Red Sox in the 1941 season.

Pitching Strategy for the Boston Braves in the Early 1950s

- Spahn and Sain, and pray for rain.

Note: During the early 1950s, Warren Spahn and Johnny Sain were the Braves' only outstanding pitchers.

When Roger Maris Broke Babe Ruth's Single-Season Record

- 61 in '61

Note: Maris hit 61 homers in 1961, breaking Ruth's record.

The Birthplace of Casey Stengel[6]

- KC

Kansas City, Missouri

Note: Stengel was a baseball player who coached the New York Yankees from 1949 to 1960.

BIOLOGY

Taxonomic Classification

- King Phillip came over for good spaghetti.
- King Phillip cooks omelets for gross slobs.
- Keep pond clean or fish get sick.
- Keep pots clean or family gets sick.
- Kind pigs care only for good slop.
- Katie put cake on Fred's good shirt.

kingdom	family
phylum	genus
class	species
order	

Human Taxonomy

- A child may promote her happiness sometimes.

CLASS	DESCRIPTION
Animalia	kingdom
Chordata	phylum
Mammalia	class
Primate	order
Hominidae	family
Homo	genus
sapiens	species

Five Biological Kingdoms

- **My promotion feels pretty awesome.**

Moneran   Plantae
Protista   Animalia
Fungi

Attributes Common to Living Things

- **MRS. GREN**

movement   reproduction
respiration   excretion
sensitivity   nutrition
growth

Cell Division: Mitosis

- **In Persia, men are tall.**

interphase   anaphase
prophase   telophase
metaphase

Stages of Prophase: Meiosis

- **Lighthearted zebras perform delightful dances.**

leptotene   diplotene
zygotene   diakinesis
pachytene

Elements Common in Living Things

- **CHON**

carbon   oxygen
hydrogen   nitrogen

The Three Most Important Groups of Mollusks

- **G**as **p**edal **c**ontrol

GROUP	EXAMPLES
Gastropoda	snails
Pelecypoda	bivalves (clams, oysters, mussels)
Cephalopoda	squids, cuttlefish, octopuses

Vertebrates

- **FARM B**

fish	mammals
amphibians	birds
reptiles	

Essential Amino Acids

There is some disagreement among scientists over the number of essential amino acids. According to the schemes presented here, arginine and histidine (included in the first device) are essential for children but not for adults. The 8 amino acids essential for adults are recalled by the second device.

- **T**hese **t**en **v**aluable **a**mino (acids) **h**ave **l**ong **p**reserved life in **m**an.

threonine	lysine
tryptophan	phenylalanine
valine	leucine
arginine	isoleucine
histidine	methionine

- **I** **l**ike **t**o **t**each **m**y **v**isitors **l**ofty **p**oliteness.

isoleucine	methionine
leucine	valine
threonine	lysine
tryptophan	phenylalanine

Five Types of Algae[7]

- **G**reen **p**ond **s**cum **s**mells **d**readful—**a**lmost **l**ike **s**auerkraut.

  GPS=green pond scum   AL=algae in lichens
  S=seaweed   S=stoneworts
  D=diatoms

One Hump or Two?

- *D* is for dromedary.
- *B* is for Bactrian.

Note: A *D* has one hump, like dromedary camels; a *B* has two humps, like Bactrian camels.

Groups in the Phylum Arthropoda

- **Ch. C. Toadi**

GROUP	EXAMPLES
Chilopoda	centipedes
Crustacea	brine shrimp, crabs, crayfish
Trilobita	trilobites (extinct)
Onychophora	peripatus
Arachnida	spiders, ticks, scorpions
Diplopoda	millipedes
Insecta	insects

Four Apes[8]

- **Go Corgi!**

  go=gorillas   or=orangutans
  c=chimpanzees   gi=gibbons

Arteries in a Frog

- Little men in short black mackintoshes

lingual	subclavian
mandibular	brachia
innominate	musculocutaneous

The Three Main Insect Body Parts

- HAT

head
abdomen
thorax

BIRTHSTONES

Birthstones (January to December)

- Great actors always develop every possible resource, perfectly seizing opportunities to tantalize.

STONE	MONTH
garnet	January
amethyst	February
aquamarine	March
diamond	April
emerald	May
pearl	June
ruby	July
peridot	August
sapphire	September
opal	October
topaz	November
turquoise	December

BOTANY

Putting Cut Flowers in Water

- The harder the stem, the hotter the water.

Evergreen Identification

- Pines come in packages.
  Firs are flat and flexible.
  Spruce are square and stiff.

  Note: Turpentine comes mainly from pine.

Wild Grass Identification

- Sedges have edges; rushes are round.

Poison Ivy Identification

- Leaflets three, let it be.

Three Species of Cedar

- Atlas cedars have ascending branches.
  Lebanon cedars have level branches.
  Deodar cedars have drooping branches.

Cutting Thistles

- Cut thistles in May, they grow in a day.
  Cut them in June, that is too soon.
  Cut them in July, then they will die.

Predicting an Early Harvest

- Mist in May, heat in June—
  Make the harvest come right soon.

Chief Constituents of Soil

- **A**ll **H**arvard **m**en **w**ant **b**ig **r**ewards.

air	water
humus	bacteria
mineral salts	rock particles

Gymnosperms (Seed Plants)

- **C**yril **s**aw **F**ern **g**et **C**onnic's **C**orvette.

cycadeoids (and cycads)	conifers
seed ferns	*Cordaites*
ginkgoes	

Stamen vs. Pistil

- sta**men**
- pist**il**

men=male part of the flower
il=g**irl**, or the female part of the flower

Trees and Shrubs with Opposite Branching[9]

- **Madc**ap **h**orse

maple	Caprifoliaceae
ash	horse chestnut
dogwood	

Note: The family Caprifoliaceae includes honeysuckles and viburnums.

Five Symptoms of Bacterial Disease in Plants[10]

- Root rot, leaf spot,
  Blight, Wilt, Gall.
  Ask me again and I'll
  Tell you them all.

The 16 Essential Elements for Plant Growth[11]

- **See Hopkins' Café managed by mine cousin Mo Clancy.**

PART OF MNEMONIC	CHEMICAL SYMBOL	CHEMICAL
see	C	carbon
hopkins	H	hydrogen
	O	oxygen
	P	phosphorus
	K	potassium
	N	nitrogen
	S	sulfur
café	Ca	calcium
	Fe	iron
managed	Mg	magnesium
by	B	boron
mine	Mn	manganese
cousin	Cu	copper
	Zn	zinc
mo	Mo	molybdenum
clancy	Cl	chlorine

CHEMISTRY AND BIOCHEMISTRY

Units of the International System of Measurement

- Many kids seeking attention keep mothers cranky.

meter	kelvin
kilogram	mole
second	candela
ampere	

Parts of an Atom

- **PEN**

  protons
  electrons
  neutrons

Note: Protons, electrons, and neutrons are positively, negatively, and neutrally (respectively) charged particles within the nucleus.

CHEMICAL SYMBOLS[12]

- Arsenic (As): "**As**sassin[s] [use] **arsenic**."
- Barium (Ba): "I like to **Ba**sk in **Ba**ths of **barium**."
- Boron (B) and Fluorine (F): "A **B** on a paper about **boron** is better than an **F** on a paper about **fluorine**."

- Calcium (Ca): "**Calcium** nurtures and baby **Ca**lves grow."
- Californium (Cf): "**C**alifornia is **f**ull of **Californium**."
- Chlorine (Cl): "**Cl**ean your pool with **chlorine**."
- Cobalt (Co): "**Co**ol **cobalt**."
- Copper (Cu): "**C u** [see you] in **Copper**town."
- Gold (Au): "**Au**stralia won the **gold** in the Olympics." "Ralph has a new **gold Au**tomobile."
- Helium (He): "**He** filled the balloons with **helium**."
- Hydrogen (H): "**H**ide from **hydrogen**."
- Iodine (I): "**I** like **iodine**."
- Iron (Fe): "**Fe**el the burn with [a hot] **iron**." "The Santa **Fe** train runs on **iron** tracks."
- Lead (Pb): "[**P**encil] **lead** [is subject to] **P**oint **b**reak."
- Magnesium (Mg): "Buy the new **MG** [car]! Made of pure **magnesium**."
- Manganese (Mn): "I have no **Mn**emonic for **manganese**."
- Mercury (Hg): "**H**orses **g**allop around **Mercury**." "One finds **H**ot **g**uys on **Mercury**."
- Neon (Ne): "**Ne**mo is a **neon** fish."
- Nickel (Ni): "**Ni**cole spent a **nickel**."
- Oxygen (O): "**O** my! That is good **oxygen**!"
- Platinum (Pt): "A **platinum Pt** Cruiser."
- Polonium (Po): "Do not mail **polonium** to the **P**ost **o**ffice."
- Potassium (K): "Does Special **K** cereal contain **potassium**?"
- Radium (Ra): "**Ra**, **Ra**, **radium**!"
- Radon (Rn): "**Radon** makes your lungs **R**eally **n**asty."
- Rhodium (Rh): "**Rh**ino **rhodium**."
- Silicon (Si): "There's nothing **si**lly about **silicon**."
- Silver (Ag): "**Silver** comes from **A**r**g**entina." "The Las Cruces **Ag**gies carry **silver** coins."
- Sodium (Na): "**Na**na bakes with too much **sodium**."
- Strontium (Sr): "**Strontium** sends off **S**trong **r**ays."
- Sulfur (S): "**Sulfur S**tinks."
- Tin (Sn): "There is **Sn**ot in the cookie **tin**."
- Tungsten (W): "Tungsten is a tongue t**W**ister." "**W**orld **W**ide **W**eb: www.**tungsten**.com."
- Xenon (Xe): "**Xe**rxes loves **xenon**."
- Zinc (Zn): "The **Zn** of **zinc**."

Elements 1–9 of the Periodic Table

- **H**enry **He**ster likes **be**er but **ca**nnot **o**btain **f**ood.

hydrogen	carbon
helium	nitrogen
lithium	oxygen
beryllium	fluorine
boron	

Elements 10–17 of the Periodic Table

- **Ne**ophyte **na**med **Mag**nolia **al**ters **si**ster's **p**hotos **s**urprisingly **cl**everly.

neon	silicon
sodium	phosphorus
magnesium	sulfur
aluminum	chlorine

The Atomic Number of Oxygen[13]

- Octa-gen

  octa=8

Note: Oxygen has an atomic number of 8, which tells you that it has 8 protons; the prefix *octa* means "eight."

The Alkali Metal Group

- **Li**ttle **Na**ncy **k**ept **rub**ies in **Ca**esar's **fr**esco.

lithium	rubidium
sodium	caseum
potassium	francium

The Alkali Earth Metals[14]

- **R**etching and **c**hoking, **B**eryl **m**anaged to **s**wallow **b**arium.

radium	magnesium
calcium	strontium
beryllium	barium

The Electromotive Series (in Order)

- **P**eople **c**an **s**eldom **m**ake **a**ny **z**wieback **i**nteresting; therefore, **l**et **h**ighly **c**lever **m**erchants **s**ell **g**ood **p**astry.

potassium	lead
calcium	hydrogen
sodium	copper
magnesium	mercury
aluminum	silver
zinc	gold
iron	platinum
tin	

The Diatomic Elements

- Honclfibr [pronounced: honkle-fibber]
- Brinclhof [pronounced: brinckle-hoff]
- **I h**ave **n**o **br**ight **o**r **cl**ever **f**riends.
- **I br**ing **cl**ay **f**or **o**ur **n**ew **h**ouse.

hydrogen	fluorine
oxygen	iodine
nitrogen	bromine
chlorine	

Oxidation and Reduction

- Oil rig: **O**xidation **i**s **l**osing (electrons), **r**eduction **i**s **g**aining (electrons).
- Elmo: **E**lectron **l**oss **m**eans **o**xidation.

- **Leo** says **ger**: Losing electrons, oxidation; gaining electrons, reduction.

Note: Oxidation is the loss of an electron by a molecule, atom, or ion; reduction is the gain of an electron by a molecule, atom, or ion.

Oxidation and Reduction: Electrodes of an Electrochemical Cell

- **O**xidation occurs at the **a**node; **r**eduction occurs at the **c**athode.

Oxidation and *anode* both start with vowels; *reduction* and *cathode* both start with consonants.

- Red cat: **Red**uction at **cat**hode.
- An ox: **An**ode for **ox**idation.

Elements Forming Hydrogen Bonds when Bonded to Hydrogen

- Hydrogen is **fon**!

  fluorine
  oxygen
  nitrogen

The Most Electronegative Elements (Descending Order of Electronegativity)

- Foncl [pronounced: phone call]

  fluorine   nitrogen
  oxygen   chlorine

Cations Are Positive

- ca+ion

   The plus sign (for positive) is reminiscent of the letter *t* in the word *cation*.

- **Cat**ions are **paws**itive.

Anions Are Negative

- An **anion** is **a** **n**egative **ion**.

Metals Form Cations in Ionic Reactions

- Metal cat, metal cat, where is my metal cat?

Ways in Which Molecules Move

- **DSO**

   diffusion
   semipermeability
   osmosis

13 Life Functions

- **I DRAG MERE CARS**.

   ingestion   response
   digestion   egestion
   reproduction   circulation
   absorption   assimilation
   growth   respiration
   movement   secretion
   excretion

The Temperature of Absolute Zero (Based on Numbers)

▪ Soon chill overtakes people totally.

Note: The number of letters in each word gives the correct answer: $-459.67°F$.

Avogadro's Number

▪ 6:02 a.m. on October 23

6.02×10^{23} atoms/mole

Note: October is the 10th month.

Charles's Law

▪ To remember Chuck, remember that if tank's too hot, you're blown into muck.

Note: The law reads: For a constant volume, the pressure of gases is directly proportional to temperature.

Henry's Law

▪ To remember good old Hank, remember the bubbles in the shaken cola you drank.

Note: The law reads: The amount of a gas dissolved in a liquid (with which it does not combine) is directly related to the partial pressure of the gas.

Boyle's Law

▪ Boyle's law is best of all because it presses gases awfully small.

Note: The law reads: The solubility of a gas increases with pressure.

DNA: Characteristics

- We love DNA,
  Made of nucleotides,
  A phosphate, sugar, and a base,
  Bonded down one side.

  Adenine and thymine,
  Make a lovely pair,
  Guanine without cytosine,
  Would be rather bare.

  Note: Sing to the tune of "Row, Row, Row Your Boat."

DNA: The Four Amine Bases

- **AT**+**GC**: **At** the **g**irl's **c**lub

  Note: Adenine pairs with thymine; guanine pairs with cytosine.

Hydrophobic Amino Acids

- **Pro gav pil**

  proline   phenylalanine
  glycine   isoleucine
  alanine   leucine
  valine

Basic Amino Acids

- **HAL**

  histidine
  arginine
  lysine

How to Dilute Sulfuric Acid Safely

- May her rest be long and placid,
  She added water to the acid.
  The other girl did what she oughter;
  She added acid to the water.

- Paw: Pour acid into water!

  Note: Sulfuric acid should be poured into water, not the other way around.

Krebs Cycle

- Can intelligent kids swiftly solve some frustrating math operations?
- Can injured kayakers safely swim for miles outdoors?

citrate   succinate
isocitrate   fumarate
ketoglutarate   malate
succinyl   oxaloacetate

Note: Also known as the citric acid cycle, the Krebs cycle represents the final steps in the oxidation of carbohydrates, fats, and proteins.

CHILDREN

- -

Checklist for Making Children Presentable[15]

- Hideous fools and morons, keep silent!

hair brushed?   knees clean?
face washed?   shoes tied (or brushed)?
middle (shirt tucked in,
   belt on)?

COOKING AND FOOD

Passing Food at the Table

- Left to right is right.

American vs. British Liquid Pints

- A pint's a pound in America all around, but a pound and a quarter of British water.

  Note: An American liquid pint equals 16 fluid ounces, but an Imperial liquid pint is 20 fluid ounces.

How to Set the Table

This mnemonic is based on the number of letters in the words for common eating utensils.

- 4 letters: *left*=fork
- 5 letters: *right*=knife and spoon

  Note: The word *left* has four letters, like *fork*; the word *right* has five letters, like *knife* and *spoon*.

How Many Teaspoons in a Tablespoon?

- One big T equals teaspoons three.

  Note: One tablespoon equals three teaspoons.

Cooking Rice

- Cooking rice? Water's twice.

  Note: Use 2 cups of water for 1 cup of rice.

Drinking Wine and Beer

- After melon, wine is felon.
- Wine upon beer, I counsel thee. Beer upon wine, let that be.
- Beer on whisky, mighty risky. Whisky on beer, never fear.

CURRENCY: AMERICAN

Portraits on American Currency (in Increasing Monetary Value)

- When juries lack honor, justice gets forgotten, making criminals miss correcting wrongs.

PORTRAIT	CURRENCY
Washington	$1
Jefferson	$2
Lincoln	$5
Hamilton	$10
Jackson	$20
Grant	$50
Franklin	$100
McKinley	$500
Cleveland	$1,000
Madison	$5,000
Chase	$10,000
Wilson	$100,000

DISTINGUISHING RIGHT FROM LEFT

Which Hand Is Which?

- Turn your hands palm downward and extend your thumbs. The letter *L* for "left" is formed by your left hand.

ELECTRONICS

Resistor Color Codes (in Order of Numerical Equivalents)

- **B**ig **b**eautiful **r**oses **o**ccupy **y**our **g**arden **b**ut **v**iolets **g**row wildly.
- **B**etter **b**e **r**ight **o**r **y**our **g**reat **b**ig **v**enture **g**oes wrong.
- **BB Roy** **g**ot **b**ack **v**ery **g**ood **w**ife.

COLOR	NUMBER
black	1
brown	2
red	3
orange	4
yellow	5
green	6
blue	7

COLOR	NUMBER
violet	8
gray	9
white	0

Note: Many mnemonic sentences have been created for remembering the resistor color codes in order by their numerical equivalents.

Ohm's Law

- **Virtuosos are rare.**

  Volts=amps×resistance

Voltage or Current Leads?

- **Eli the ice man.**

  E=voltage   I=current
  L=inductance   C=capacitor

Note: Voltage leads current in an inductance circuit; current leads voltage in a capacitor circuit.

Power

- **PIE**

  Power=current×voltage

Note: The symbol for power is P, the symbol for current is I, and the symbol for voltage is E.

Converters and Inverters

- **CAD**: Converters change **AC** to **DC**.
- **IDA**: Inverters change **DC** to **AC**.

Fleming's Rules: Which Hand?

- Gene**right**or

  Use Fleming's right-hand rules for generators.

  Note: Thus, use Fleming's left-hand rules for motors. Fleming's rules pertain to the relationship between motion and magnetic field.

ENGLISH GRAMMAR AND PRONUNCIATION

Nine Parts of Speech

- Three little words you often see
  Are articles—**a, an**, and **the**.
  A noun's the name of anything;
  As **school** or **garden**, **hoop**, or **swing**.
  Adjectives tell the kind of noun;
  As **great**, **small**, **pretty**, **white**, or **brown**.
  Instead of nouns the pronouns stand;
  Her head, **his** face, **our** arms, **your** hand.
  Verbs tell of something being done;
  To **read**, **count**, **sing**, **laugh**, **jump**, or **run**.
  How things are done the adverbs tell;
  As **slowly**, **quickly**, **ill**, or **well**.
  Conjunctions join the words together;
  As men **and** women, wind **or** weather.
  The preposition stands before
  A noun, as **in** or **through** a door.
  The interjections show surprise;

As, **oh**! how pretty, **ah**! how wise!
The whole are called nine parts of speech.
Which reading, writing, speaking teach.

Types of Sentences[16]

- Declarative sentences all make a statement:
  I visited my cousin.
  Clouds are in the sky.
  Declarative sentences all make a statement:
  Today is Friday.
  We hope to bake a pie.
  Interrogative sentences all ask a question:
  Where is your raincoat?
  Do you know the time?
  Interrogative sentences all ask a question:
  When will the game start?
  Did you lose a dime?
  Imperative sentences all give an order:
  Open the door, please.
  Stay here a while.
  Imperative sentences all give an order:
  Please call him later.
  Look at me and smile.
  Exclamatory sentences express strong emotion:
  Wow! That's amazing!
  Thanks! You're a dear!
  Exclamatory sentences express strong emotion:
  What a good story!
  I can't believe you're here!

  Note: Sing to the tune of "Down by the Station."

Fewer vs. Less

- Because *fewer* describes countable things and *less* what can't be counted, you can have **fewer sewer**s but **less** stress.

Parts of Speech (without Articles and Interjections)

▪ **V**iolet **a**dopts **a**ging **c**ats **n**eeding **p**ersonal **p**rotection.

verb
adjective
adverb
conjunction

noun
preposition
pronoun

Coordinating Conjunctions

▪ **BOY SAT** with **BEN**

but
or
yet
so
and

then
both . . . and
either . . . or
neither . . . nor

Note: Coordinating conjunctions combine grammatical units of equal status.

Affect vs. Effect

▪ Raven: **R**emember **a**ffect **v**erb **e**ffect **n**oun.

Note: This mnemonic works for the most common usages of the two words. In psychology and psychiatry, however, *affect* can be used as a noun to describe feelings or emotions (as when a patient displays diminished affect). Sometimes *effect* is used as a verb, meaning "to bring about" (to effect change).

How to Pronounce *Mnemosyne*[17]

▪ Mnemosyne had two knees.

Knee-mahs-n-knee

Note: Mnemosyne was the goddess of memory.

How to Pronounce *Quay*

- When by a quay,
  Think of the sea.
  And don't say "kay,"
  Say "key."

  Note: A quay is a wharf.

How to Pronounce *Asterisk*[18]

- Mary had an aeroplane,
  About the clouds to frisk.
  Now wasn't she a silly thing,
  Her little *.

  Note: An asterisk is the symbol "*."

The Four Words Ending in *-efy*

- **Rare students pursue lists.**

  rarefy   putrefy
  stupefy   liquefy

The Three Present-Tense Verbs Ending in *-ceed*

- **Ex-pro succeeds.**

  exceed
  proceed
  succeed

The Four Most Common Words Ending in *-yze*

- **CAPE**

  catalyze   paralyze
  analyze   electrolyze

FISHING

How the Wind Affects Fishing[19]

- When the wind is in the East,
  It's neither good for man nor beast.
  When the wind is in the North,
  The skillful fisher goes not forth.
  When the wind is in the South,
  It blows the bait in the fish's mouth.
  When the wind is in the West,
  Then it is at its very best.

How to Catch a Trout[20]

- The rod light and taper, thy tackle fine,
  Thy lead ten inches upon the line;
  Bigger or less, according to the stream,
  Angle in the dark, when others dream:
  Or in a cloudy day with a lively worm,
  The Bradlin is best; but give him a turn
  Before thou do land a large well grown trout.
  And if with a fly thou wilt have a bout,
  Overload not with links, that the fly may fall
  First on the stream for that's all in all.
  The line shorter than the rod, with a natural fly:
  But the chief point of all is the cookery.

GAMES

Chess

- White is right.

  When beginning a chess game, the square of each player's right-hand corner should be white.

- Queen is on her own color.

  The white queen should be on a white square, and the black queen on a black square.

- 1-2-3, R'n'B!

  The rooks/castles (R) are on the corners (1), the knights (n) are next to rooks (2), and bishops (B) are on the next square in (3).

Bridge: Ranking of Suits for Bidding

- **N**ever **s**hould **h**obbies **d**ivide **c**ouples.

  no trump   diamonds
  spade   clubs
  heart

Poker: Sequence of Winning Hands[21]

HAND	DEVICE
straight flush	13 letters
four of a kind	11 letters
full house	9 letters
flush	5 letters
straight	
three-of-a-kind	three
two pair	two
one pair	one
high card	

Note: The "F" hands all come together, and the number of letters gives the order (except for the royal flush, the highest hand—not shown). The "number" hands can be remembered by their sequence: three, two, and one.

Snooker: Order of Balls in Back Court (Left to Right)

- **G**od **b**less **y**ou.

COLOR	POINTS
green	3 points
brown	4 points
yellow	2 points

Snooker: Order for Plotting Colors after Last Ball Is Placed (Start of Frame)

- **Y**ou **g**o **b**rown **b**efore **p**inky **b**links.

yellow	blue
green	pink
brown	black

GEOGRAPHY

How to Spell *Geography*

- **G**eorge **E**liot's **o**ld **g**randmother **r**ode **a** **p**ig **h**ome **y**esterday.

Longitude vs. Latitude

- **Long**itude

  Long lines run pole to pole.

- **Lat**s are flat.
- **La**dder

  Latitude lines run horizontally around the globe.

The Tropics: Cancer or Capricorn?

- **Ca**ncer

  N for north of the equator.

- Farther down the alphabet, farther down on the globe

  Capricorn comes after *Cancer* in the dictionary; it is south of the equator.

Time Zones in the World

- Number of hours in a day: 24

Landforms[22]

- **Chorus**
  Our land has landforms,
  Or special features,
  This land is home to
  So many creatures.
  All kinds of landforms
  Are found around the world.
  Landforms make up our special land!

  Up in the highlands,
  You'll find the mountains;
  Plus hills and cliffs
  And flat-top mesas.
  These lands are highlands,
  A special feature.
  Landforms make up our special land!
  [Chorus]
  Down in the lowlands,
  You'll find the canyons,
  Plus river valleys,
  And bluffs and gorges.
  These lands are lowlands,
  A special feature.
  Landforms make up our special land!
  [Chorus]
  Deep in the wetlands
  Are swamps and marshes,
  Plus soggy bogs
  With lots of water.
  These lands are wetlands,
  A special feature.
  Landforms make up our special land!
  [Chorus]
  Across the plains
  It's mostly treeless.
  The land is flat
  With grasses growing.

These lands are plains,
A special feature.
Landforms make up our special land!
[Chorus]

Note: Sing to the tune of "This Land Is Your Land."

U.S. Regions[23]

- The U.S.A.
  Is divided into regions,
  Seven main regions
  In the U.S.A.
  New England, Midatlantic,
  Southern, Midwestern,
  Rocky Mountain, Southwestern,
  Pacific Coast. Hey!

  The New England states are:
  Connecticut, Maine,
  Massachusetts, New Hampshire,
  Rhode Island, and Vermont.
  The Midatlantic states are:
  New York and New Jersey,
  Plus Pennsylvania.
  What more could you want?

  The Southern states are:
  Delaware, Florida,
  Maryland, Kentucky,
  Mississippi, Alabama,
  Arkansas, Tennessee,
  Virginia, West Virginia,
  North Carolina, South Carolina,
  Georgia, Louisiana.

  The Midwestern states are:
  Kansas, Nebraska,
  Iowa, Illinois,
  Ohio, Minnesota,

Michigan, Missouri,
Wisconsin, Indiana,
North Dakota,
And South Dakota.

And Rocky Mountain states are:
Idaho, Nevada,
Montana, Wyoming,
Utah, Colorado.

The Southwestern states are:
Texas, Arizona,
New Mexico, and
Oklahoma.

The Pacific Coast states are:
California, Washington,
And then Oregon.
That's 48. Hey!

The last two states,
Alaska and Hawaii,
Are in other areas
Further away.

Note: Sing to the tune of "This Land Is Your Land."

The Continents

- **Eat an as**pirin **after a north**ern **sou**p.

Europe	Australia
Antartica	North America
Asia	South America
Africa	

The Continents (in Order of Decreasing Size)

- **As af**fluent **Nor**man **s**ued **An**dy, **Au**rora **e**vacuated.

Asia	Antarctica
Africa	Australia
North America	Europe
South America	

Largest Continent

- Shortest name equals largest land mass.

Asia

Four Oceans

- **I** am **a** person.

| Indian | Arctic |
| Atlantic | Pacific |

Note: This mnemonic excludes the Southern Ocean (also known as the South Polar Ocean and the Antarctic Ocean).

Four Oceans (in Order of Descending Size)

- **P**lease **a**llow **I**ndian **a**rt.

| Pacific | Indian |
| Atlantic | Arctic |

Note: This mnemonic excludes the Southern Ocean (also known as the South Polar Ocean and the Antarctic Ocean).

The Five Oceans (in Order of Descending Size)

- **PAISA**
- **P**aul **a**vidly **i**nsults **s**outherners **a**rticulately.

Pacific	Southern
Atlantic	Arctic
Indian	

The Great Lakes

- **HOMES**

Huron	Erie
Ontario	Superior
Michigan	

The Great Lakes: From West to East

- **S**ee **M**r. **H**uron **e**ating **o**ranges.

Superior	Erie
Michigan	Ontario
Huron	

The Great Lakes: From East to West

- **O**nly **e**lephants **h**ave **m**assive **s**nouts.

Ontario	Michigan
Erie	Superior
Huron	

The Great Lakes (in Order of Descending Surface Area)

- **S**am's **h**orse **m**ust **e**at **o**ats.

Superior	Erie
Huron	Ontario
Michigan	

States Bordering the Great Lakes[24]

- **I'M NO WIMP.**

Indiana	Wisconsin
Michigan	Illinois
New York	Minnesota
Ohio	Pennsylvania

The Two Great Lakes Next to Niagara Falls (from West to East)

- **LENOR**

   Left—Erie—Niagara—Ontario—Right

The Great Lakes in Both America and Canada

- **SHOE**

   Superior   Ontario
   Huron   Erie

The Seven Hills of Rome

- **Q**ueen **V**ictoria **c**ould **e**ntertain **p**eople **a**lways **c**ompletely.

   Quirinal   Palatine
   Viminal   Aventine
   Capitoline   Caelian
   Esquiline

The Counties of Northern Ireland[25]

- **A**lways **a** **d**readful **l**and **f**or **t**rouble
- **FAT LAD**

   Antrim   Londonderry
   Armagh   Fermanagh
   Down   Tyrone

The British Isles

- **WISE**

   Wales   Scotland
   Ireland   England

New York City: Numbered Streets[26]

- Eastbound streets are even.
  Westbound streets are odd.
  Obey the traffic signals
  And leave the rest to God.

The Four Corners

- **CANU**

Colorado	New Mexico
Arizona	Utah

Note: The Four Corners is the point at which the borders of these four states meet.

Countries of Central America (from North to South)

- **B**etter **g**o **h**ome **e**very **n**ight **c**ompletely **p**aid.

Belize	Nicaragua
Guatemala	Costa Rica
Honduras	Panama
El Salvador	

Provinces of Canada[27]

- **N**ewly **s**tructured **q**uadrangles **b**y **c**ourteous **Mr. PEI a**ttract **n**ew **b**uyers **n**eeding **o**ffice **s**pace.

Nova Scotia	Alberta
Quebec	New Brunswick
British Columbia	Newfoundland
Manitoba	Ontario
Prince Edward Island	Saskatchewan

Note: On December 6, 2001, Newfoundland officially became Newfoundland and Labrador.

Territories of Canada (before 1999)

- Why TNT?

MNEMONIC	ABBREVIATION	TERRITORY
Why T	YT	Yukon Territories
NT	NT	Northwest Territories

Note: On April 1, 1999, Canada admitted a third territory, Nunavut, which was formed from what was part of the Northwest Territories.

Territories of Canada (after 1999)

- Why TNT? I'll have Nunavut.

Train Stops on the Original Main Line out of Philadelphia

- Old maids never wed and have babies.

Overbrook	Ardmore
Merion	Haverford
Narberth	Bryn Mawr
Wynnewood	

Seattle: East–West Streets of Southern Downtown (in Pairs)

- Jesus Christ made Seattle under protest.

J=Jefferson and James	S=Spring and Seneca
C=Cherry and Columbia	U=University and Union
M=Marion and Madison	P=Pike and Pine

The Five Smallest Countries (in Order of Ascending Size)

- Very minute nations to see

COUNTRY	SIZE (IN SQUARE MILES)
Vatican City	0.16
Monaco	0.73
Nauru	8
Tuvalu	9.25
San Marino	24

The Countries across Northern Africa (from West to East)[28]

- **MALE** around Tunisia

Morocco	Libya
Algeria	Egypt

Note: Tunisia lies between Algeria and Libya.

Cape of Good Hope vs. Cape Horn[29]

- **ABC'FGH**

African	of ('F)
bottom	Good
Cape	Hope

Note: The Cape of Good Hope is in Africa, and Cape Horn is in South America.

The Two Land-Locked Countries of South America

- **P**acific **b**locked

Paraguay
Bolivia

Netherlands Islands off the Coast of Venezuela

- **ABC**

  Aruba
  Bonaire
  Curacao

Districts/States of Pakistan

- **Pak*i*stan**

Punjab	Sindh
Afghan	Baluchistan
Kashmir	

  Note: Pakistan was named after these districts or states in 1933.

The Nine Largest Islands in the World[30]

- **Green Guineas born mad baff**le some **h**onest **great British** vicars.

Green=Greenland	s=Sumatra
Guineas=New Guinea	h=Honshu
born=Borneo	great British=Great Britain
mad=Madagascar	v=Victoria
baff=Baffin	

  Note: This mnemonic excludes Australia, which is a continent.

The Two American States Adjacent to the Most Other States[31]

- **T**ouches **m**ost

  Tennessee
  Missouri

  Note: These states each border 8 other states.

States Surrounding Texas

- **LOAN**

Louisiana   Arkansas
Oklahoma   New Mexico

The Ten Largest American States (in Decreasing Order)

- **A**l's **t**aking **C**arl **m**ountain climbing **n**ext **M**onday **a**fter **N**ed **c**opes **w**ith **o**bjections.

Alaska   Arizona
Texas   Nevada
California   Colorado
Montana   Wyoming
New Mexico   Oregon

The American States with the Longest Coastlines (in Decreasing Order)

- **A**lways **f**old **C**al's **h**abiliments **l**ast.

Alaska   Hawaii
Florida   Louisiana
California

The Five Smallest American States (in Increasing Order)

- **R**alph **d**elivered **C**onnie's **n**ew **j**ersey **n**ear **H**ampton.

Rhode Island   New Jersey
Delaware   New Hampshire
Connecticut

GEOLOGY

Earth's Crust: The Most Abundant Elements (in Sequence by Percent of Total Weight)

The first mnemonic device is based on the names of the elements; the second is based on the symbols of the elements.

- **O**nly **s**illy **a**sses **I**n **c**ollege **s**tudy **p**ast **m**idnight.
- **O**nly **s**illy **A**lvin **f**ears **ca**nnibalizing **N**athan **K**elly's **MG.**

ELEMENT	SYMBOL
oxygen	O
silicon	Si
aluminum	Al
iron	Fe
calcium	Ca
sodium	Na
potassium	K
magnesium	Mg

Geologic Timescale (Periods)

- **C**amels **o**ften **s**it **d**own **c**arefully. **P**erhaps **t**heir **j**oints **c**reak. **P**ossibly **e**arly **o**iling **m**ight **p**revent **p**ermanent **r**heumatism.

Cambrian	Cretaceous
Ordovician	Paleocene
Silurian	Eocene
Devonian	Oligocene
Carboniferous	Miocene
Permian period	Pliocene
Triassic	Pleistocene
Jurassic	Recent

Note: The first and last periods of the Paleozoic Era are the Cambrian and Permian, respectively. The first and last periods of the Mesozoic Era are the Triassic and Cretaceous, respectively. The first period of the Cenozoic Era (our current era) is the Paleocene.

Mohs Hardness Scale for Minerals (in Increasing Order of Hardness)

- **T**all **g**irls **c**an **f**ight **a**nd **o**rder **q**ueens **t**o **c**arry **d**iamonds.

MINERAL	RELATIVE HARDNESS
talc	1
gypsum	2
calcite	3
fluorite	4
apatite	5
orthoclase	6
quartz	7
topaz	8
corundum	9
diamond	10

GEOPOLITICS

The G8 Countries[32]

- **Can U JIG** (with) **R**ussia's **K**ing **Fran**?

Canada	Germany
United States	Russia
Japan	United Kingdom (King)
Italy	France

Members of OPEC

- **LIV A QUIK SIN**

Libya	Indonesia
Iran	Kuwait
Venezuela	Saudi Arabia
Algeria	Iraq
Qatar	Nigeria
United Arab Emirates	

Note: OPEC is an acronym for Organization of Petroleum-Exporting Countries.

GERMAN

Pronunciation of the Combination *IE*[33]

- When I and E go walking, the E does the talking.
  But when E precedes I from the rear, it's the latter that you hear.

Note: In German, *IE* is pronounced "ee" and *EI* is pronounced "eye." Examples: *Friede* (which means "peace") and *drei* (which means "three").

Propositions Governing the Dative Case[34]

- Rose are red
  Violets are blue,
  Aus, bei, mit, nach,
  seit, von, zu.

German Definite Articles[35]

- Oh the masculine changes from *der* to *den*,
  And the feminine, neuter, and plural stay the same.
  In the dative case it's really a shame,
  Its *dem*, *der*, *dem*, and the plural is *den*.

  Look at the genitive, see what it does.
  Look at the genitive, see what it has.
  It's *des*, *der*, *des*, *der*—
  Whoever has something hasn't a care.

  Note: Sing to the tune of "Turkey in the Straw."

CASE	MASCULINE	FEMININE	NEUTER	PLURAL
Nominative	*der*	*die*	*das*	*die*
Genitive	*des*	*der*	*des*	*der*
Dative	*dem*	*der*	*dem*	*den*
Accusative	*den*	*die*	*das*	*die*

HISTORY: AMERICAN

Year Columbus Discovered America

- In fourteen hundred and ninety-two, Columbus sailed the ocean blue.

Civil War: Year Began

- When the North the South did shun, 'twas eighteen hundred sixty-one.

Civil War: Year Ended

- When the union did survive, twas eighteen hundred sixty-five.

Civil War: Uniforms

- Blue=Union
- Gray=Confederacy

Original 13 Colonies (in Order of Admission)[36]

- Del, Penn, NJ
  Led the way.
  George, Conn, Mass—
  Next in class.
  Seven, Mary;
  Eight, South Carrie.
  New Hamp, nine on
  The founding state.
  Virginia, ten;
  New York was late.
  NC, RI,
  They cast the die
  And saved the day
  For the USA.

Delaware	South Carolina
Pennsylvania	New Hampshire
New Jersey	Virginia
Georgia	New York
Connecticut	North Carolina
Massachusetts	Rhode Island
Maryland	

American Revolution: Important Years[37]

- **LIBERTY**, 1775–1781

EVENT	YEAR
Battle of **L**exington	1775
Declaration of **I**ndependence	1776
Burgoyne surrenders	1777
Evacuation of Philadelphia	1778
*Bonhomme **R**ichard* naval victory	1779
Treason of Benedict Arnold	1780
Battle and treaty at **Y**orktown	1781

States of the Confederacy[38]

- **T**en friends were in an **ar**k: two **Carols**, **Ginny**, **Miss Flora**, **George**, **Tex**, **Al**, and **Lou**, then who?

Tennessee	Florida
Arkansas	Georgia
South Carolina	Texas
North Carolina	Alabama
Virginia	Louisiana
Mississippi	

AMENDMENTS TO THE CONSTITUTION[39]

Amendment 1

- **RAPPOS***

religion	press
assembly	opinion
petition	speech

Note: The First Amendment protects the freedoms of religion, assembly, petition, press, opinion, and speech.

Amendment 2

- 2 arms; I have the right 2 bear arms, not to arm bears.*

Note: The Second Amendment states that citizens have the right to bear arms.

Amendment 3

- No housing troops*

That device has 3 words.

Note: The Third Amendment protects people from being forced to house military troops in peacetime. The British had forced the colonists to house troops.

Amendment 4

- What are you looking for [4]*?
- Search 4 something.

Note: The Fourth Amendment protects citizens against unreasonable searches and seizures of property.

Amendment 5

- I am standing on the Fifth.*

Note: The Fifth Amendment protects citizens from being forced to testify against themselves. The amendment also protects citizens from double jeopardy—that is, once one has been acquitted of a crime, one cannot be tried a second time for that same crime.

Amendment 6

- Public speedy trials*

Each word has 6 letters.

Note: The Sixth Amendment entitles citizens accused of a crime to a speedy and public trial.

Amendment 7

- Lucky 7*

Note: The Seventh Amendment protects a right to a trial by jury in civil cases involving more than $20. For many people, having a jury trial will increase their luck in getting a favorable decision.

Amendment 8

- Fair bail*
- Fair fine*

Each of these devices has 8 letters.

- My horse 8 a "bail" of hay.*

Note: The Eighth Amendment requires fair bail and fines and prohibits cruel and unusual punishment.

Amendment 9

- 9 is a backward *P* for power and people.

Note: The Ninth Amendment asserts that the enumeration (specific listing) of individual rights in the Constitution does not deny or disparage other rights retained by the people. In short, this amendment implies that citizens have rights not explicitly mentioned in the Constitution.

Amendment 10

- State right.

That device contains 10 letters.

Note: The Tenth Amendment asserts that powers not explicitly delegated to the federal government by the Constitution or prohibited to the states are reserved to the states or the people. The amendment is sometimes called "the states' rights amendment" because it explicitly warrants divisions of power between states and the federal government.

Amendment 11

- One (1) citizen may not sue in federal court one (1) state that isn't one's own without that state court's permission.[*]

Note: The Eleventh Amendment prohibits, say, a resident of Virginia from suing the state of North Carolina without permission from the state court of North Carolina.

Amendment 12

- One (1) must have two (2) sets of electoral ballots: one for the president and one for the vice president.

Note: The Twelfth Amendment deals with how we once elected the president, and required separate ballots for the president and the vice president.

Amendment 13

- Freed the slave
- Emancipations

Each of these devices has 13 letters.

- 13 is unlucky for most, but was lucky for slaves.*
- The 13 colonies were liberated; the 13th Amendment liberated the slaves.*

Note: The Thirteenth Amendment abolished slavery as an institution.

Amendment 14

- "Foreignteen-born" and native-born have the same rights.*

Note: The Fourteenth Amendment asserts that all citizens, native-born or naturalized, have the same rights and that due process rights of the Fifth Amendment apply also to state governments.

Amendment 15

- Every man may vote.

That device has 15 letters.

Note: The Fifteenth Amendment extended voting rights to all adult males, including all black males, regardless of whether they were once slaves.

Amendment 16

- Pay tax to Uncle Sam.

That device has 16 letters.

- Sweet 16: Lots of money.

Note: The Sixteenth Amendment instituted the federal income tax.

Amendment 17

- Elect your senators.

That device has 17 letters.

Note: The Seventeenth Amendment calls for the popular election of senators for six-year terms and specifies procedures for filling vacancies in the Senate. Before that amendment, senators were appointed by state legislators.

Amendment 18

- You can't drink at 18.*

Note: The Eighteenth Amendment instituted alcohol prohibition, forbidding the manufacture, sale, or transportation of "intoxicating liquors."

Amendment 19

- All ladies may now vote.

That device has 19 letters.

- 19 ladies went out to vote.*

Note: The Nineteenth Amendment extended voting rights to women.

Amendment 20

- The president takes office on January 20.*

Note: The Twentieth Amendment moved the presidential inauguration to January 20. It used to be on March 4. The amendment also sets the date for inaugurating Congress (January 3) and specifies the procedures to be followed if the president-elect dies or no president has been chosen or qualified by the beginning of the presidential term.

Amendment 21

- At 21, people may now drink.*

Note: The Twenty-First Amendment repealed the Eighteenth Amendment, ending alcohol prohibition. It was the first amendment designed to repeal another amendment.

Amendment 22

- 22=2 terms*
- 2 limit to 2 terms*

Note: The Twenty-Second Amendment limits a president's tenure to two terms.

Amendment 23

- DC will vote now for the Prez.

That device has 23 letters.

- 2+3=5

The Pentagon (associated with Washington, DC, though in Arlington, Virginia) has 5 sides.

Note: The Twenty-Third Amendment allows the residents of Washington, D.C., to vote in presidential elections.

Amendment 24

- The busiest place on Earth on Dec. 24 is the North Pole, which will be abbreviated to No Pol.*

Note: The Twenty-Fourth Amendment prohibits charging people for registering to vote.

Amendment 25

- The 25th President (McKinley) was killed in office.[*]

Note: The Twenty-Fifth Amendment sets procedures for replacing a president because of removal from office, disability, or death.

Amendment 26

- $26 - (2 + 6) = 18$

Note: The Twenty-Sixth Amendment lowered the voting age to 18.

Amendment 27

- Highest amendment number = highest salary[*]

Note: The Twenty-Seventh Amendment requires congressional pay raises to take effect only after an intervening election, disabling members of Congress from giving themselves raises in current terms.

The Bill of Rights (in Order)[40]

- **REQUISITES** for freedom

  religious and other freedoms (assembly, speech, the press)
  establishment of a militia and the right to bear arms
  quartering of troops prohibited
  unreasonable search and seizure prohibited
  incrimination of self prohibited
  speedy public and impartial trial guaranteed
  indictments over $20 have a right to trial by jury
  too much bail, excessive fines, and cruel punishment
    prohibited
  enumeration of certain rights doesn't deny others
  states or the people reserve all powers not explicitly
    enumerated for the federal government

The 16th to 19th Amendments to the Constitution (in Order)[41]

- **In come senators** with **wine** and **women**.

AMENDMENT	PROVISION
16th	federal income tax
17th	direct election of senators
18th	prohibition of the sale, manufacture, and distribution of alcohol
19th	voting rights for women

PRESIDENTS OF THE UNITED STATES

1. George Washington, 1789–1797
2. John Adams, 1797–1801
3. Thomas Jefferson, 1801–1809
4. James Madison, 1809–1817
5. James Monroe, 1817–1825
6. John Quincy Adams, 1825–1829
7. Andrew Jackson, 1829–1837
8. Martin Van Buren, 1837–1841
9. William Henry Harrison, 1841
10. John Tyler, 1841–1845
11. James Knox Polk, 1845–1849
12. Zachary Taylor, 1849–1850
13. Millard Fillmore, 1850–1853
14. Franklin Pierce, 1853–1857
15. James Buchanan, 1857–1861
16. Abraham Lincoln, 1861–1865
17. Andrew Johnson, 1865–1869
18. Ulysses Simpson Grant, 1869–1877
19. Rutherford Birchard Hayes, 1877–1881
20. James Abram Garfield, 1881
21. Chester Alan Arthur, 1881–1885

22. Grover Cleveland, 1885–1889
23. Benjamin Harrison, 1889–1893
24. Grover Cleveland, 1893–1897
25. William McKinley, 1897–1901
26. Theodore Roosevelt, 1901–1909
27. William Howard Taft 1909–1913
28. Woodrow Wilson, 1913–1921
29. Warren Gamaliel Harding, 1921–1923
30. Calvin Coolidge, 1923–1929
31. Herbert Clark Hoover, 1929–1933
32. Franklin Delano Roosevelt, 1933–1945
33. Harry S Truman, 1945–1953
34. Dwight David Eisenhower, 1953–1961
35. John Fitzgerald Kennedy, 1961–1963
36. Lyndon Baines Johnson, 1963–1969
37. Richard Milhous Nixon, 1969–1974
38. Gerald Rudolph Ford, 1974–1977
39. James Earl Carter Jr., 1977–1981
40. Ronald Wilson Reagan, 1981–1989
41. George Herbert Walker Bush, 1989–1993
42. William Jefferson Clinton, 1993–2001
43. George Walker Bush, 2001–2009

Presidents: 1–11 (in Order)

- **W**ashington's **a**rmy **j**ogged **m**any **m**iles **a**nd **j**ogged **v**ery **h**ard **t**o **P**hiladelphia.

Presidents: 12–25 (in Order)

- **T**o **f**ind **p**retty **B**ritish **l**adies, **J**ohnson **g**ave **H**ayes **g**arish **a**nd **c**lever **h**eart-shaped **c**lay **m**aps.

Presidents 26–42 (Presidents of the 20th Century in Order)

- **T**heodore **t**akes **W**ilson's **h**and, **c**oolly **h**ooting **F**ranklin's **t**rue **e**xperiences. **K**en **j**ustly **n**ixed **F**ord's **c**ar, **r**ated **B**ush **c**linker.

Presidents 1–40 (through Reagan, in Order)[42]

- Georgie, Adams, Jeff, and Mad.
  James Monroe, John Quincy Ad.
  Andy Jack and M. Van B.,
  William Hen, Ty, Polk, Z. T.
  Mill Fill and Pierce, Buch and Abe,
  Johnson, Grant, Rutherford Hayes.
  Garfield, Chet, next Grover C.,
  Before and after Harrison, B.
  McKin, T. R., W. H. Taft,
  Wilson, Harding, Cal—no laugh.
  Herbert Hoover, FDR,
  Harry Truman, Eisenhower.
  Kennedy and LBJ,
  Dick, Ford, Jimmy, and Ron Rea.

Presidents: 14th

- Franklin Pierce = fourteenth president

Presidents Assassinated in Office

- Loony gunmen maliciously killed.

Lincoln	McKinley
Garfield	Kennedy

Rule or Curse of 20

All but one American president who died in office was elected between 1840 and 1960 in a year divisible by 20. The only exception to this rule was Zachary Taylor, who died on July 9, 1850.

ELECTED	NAME	DATE DIED	CAUSE
1840	William Harrison	April 4, 1841	pneumonia
1860	Abraham Lincoln	April 15, 1865	shot by John Wilkes Booth
1880	James Garfield	September 19, 1881	shot by Charles J. Guiteau
1900	William McKinley	September 14, 1901	shot by Leon Czolgosz
1920	Warren Harding	August 2, 1923	possible heart attack or stroke
1940	Franklin Roosevelt	April 12, 1945	cerebral hemorrhage
1960	John Kennedy	November 22, 1963	shot by Lee Harvey Oswald

CAMPAIGN SLOGANS

Political slogans can be used as mnemonic devices to help remember candidates, running mates, and issues.

The Campaign of 1840

- Tippecanoe and Tyler too!

The slogan was used by the Whig Party when William Henry Harrison, hero of the Battle of Tippecanoe, was the party's presidential candidate and John Tyler was his running mate.

The Campaign of 1884

- A public office is a public trust.

The Democrats used the slogan to remind voters that James G. Blaine, the Republican candidate, was believed to have sold favors to a railroad while Blaine was Speaker of the House in the 1870s.

- Ma, Ma, Where's my paw? Gone to the White House. Haw, haw, haw.

The slogan was used by Republican Blaine to remind the voters that Grover Cleveland, Blaine's opponent and a bachelor, had admitted during the campaign to fathering a child out of wedlock.

- Blaine, Blaine. James G. Blaine. The continental liar from the state of Maine.

The Democrats countered the Republican attacks on Cleveland's fathering a child out of wedlock with this slogan attacking Blaine's honesty.

The Campaign of 1904

- A man, a plan, a canal, Panama.

Teddy Roosevelt used this slogan to present the issue of the construction of the Panama Canal. The slogan is also a famous palindrome, which reads the same backward and forward.

The Campaign of 1936

- Up with Alf—Down with the alphabet.

This slogan is from Alf Landon, who ran against Franklin Roosevelt, who was seeking his second term. The slogan was an attack on the numerous "alphabet agencies" (such as the WPA, SEC, and TVA) set up in FDR's first term.

Cabinet Secretaries (in Order of Creation and Succession; Current)

- See the dog jump in a circle; leave her home to entertain every visitor here.

state	health and human services
treasury	housing and urban
defense	development
justice	transportation
interior	energy
agriculture	education
commerce	veteran's affairs
labor	homeland security

Presidential Cabinet (about 1940)

- **ST. WAPNIACL**

state	navy
treasury	interior
war	agriculture
attorney general	commerce
postmaster general	labor

Civil Rights: Personalities[43]

- Tell me, who fought the fights?
  Who promoted civil rights?
  Who devoted days and nights
  Working hard for rights?
  Who rose to the heights
  In the struggle for rights,
  For civil rights?

  Harriett Tubman was brave,
  Freeing many a slave.
  The Underground Railroad
  She helped to pave.

She risked her life
In order to save
People's civil rights!

Sojourner Truth, you see,
Opposed slavery.
This former slave
Spoke for equality.
Her message reached
The White House in D.C.
"We want civil rights!"

Frederick Douglass, so bright,
Was a true, guiding light.
An important newspaper
He did write.
He urged his readers
All to unite
For civil rights!

Dr. Martin Luther King
Did many a great thing.
He preached and said,
"Let freedom ring!"
He marched to spread
His inspiring dream
Of civil rights!

Note: Sing to the tune of "Do Your Ears Hang Low?"

Women's Rights[44]

- **Chorus**
  Special women,
  Special women,
  Special women,
  You fought for women's rights.

Determined, how you rolled along,
Spoke out strong, led the throng.
Working hard to right each wrong,
You fought for women's rights.
[Chorus]
How you worked so tirelessly,
Susan B. Anthony,
Leading protests just to see
That women got the vote.
Elizabeth Cady Stanton, too.
Women owe lots to you.
At conferences, you shared your view
That women must have rights.
[Chorus]
Cheers go to Lucretia Mott,
For organizing quite a lot.
And, Lucy Stone, no one forgot
Your talks on women's rights.
Hooray for Carrie Chapman Catt.
Give a cheer! Tip your hat!
Celebrate the women that
Fought hard for women's rights!
[Chorus]

Note: Sing to the tune of "Goodnight, Ladies."

Colleges of the Ivy League

- **P**reppy **p**eople **c**ompete **h**ere **c**ollegially, **y**et **d**elight **b**ankers.

Princeton	Columbia
Penn (University of Pennsylvania)	Yale Dartmouth
Cornell	Brown
Harvard	

Colleges of the Seven Sisters

- Barbara Smith made vast wealth before retiring.

Barnard	Wellesley
Smith	Bryn Mawr
Mount Holyoke	Radcliffe
Vassar	

HISTORY: BRITISH

Battle of Hastings

- William the Conqueror, ten sixty-six,
  Played on the Saxons oft-cruel tricks.

Defeat of the Spanish Armada: Year

- The Spanish armada met its fate in fifteen hundred eighty-eight.

Civil War: Decisive Battle

- In sixteen hundred and forty-four,
  They fought the battle of Marston Moor.

Roundheads vs. Cavaliers[45]

- Roundheads followed Cromwell.
- Cavaliers followed Charles I.

Sides in the War of the Roses[46]

- **White** Plains, New **York**.

The white rose was the emblem of the House of York.

Note: The red rose was the emblem of the House of Lancaster.

ROYALTY AND THE PEERAGE

Henry VIII: Wives (in Chronological Order)

- Cat of A, Anne Bo, and Jane See,
  Anne of Clee, Cat Ho, and Cat P:
  These three Cats, two Annes and a Jane
  Were attracted by Hal to their bane.

Catherine of Aragon	Anne of Cleves
Anne Boleyn	Catherine Howard
Jane Seymour	Catherine Parr

Henry VIII: Fate of Wives (in Chronological Order)

- Divorced, beheaded, died,
  Divorced, beheaded, survived.

Note: See previous list for Henry VIII's wives' names.

George III: Year of Accession

- George the third said with a smile, "Seventeen-sixty yards in a mile."

Note: Indeed, there are 1,760 yards in a mile.

Charles II: Ministers

- **CABAL**

Clifford	Ashley-Cooper
Arlington	Lauderdale
Buckingham	

Note: Lauderdale signed a treaty with France against Holland in 1672. The acronym *CABAL* became popular in the English language as word in its own right, though the word *cabal* existed before that time.

The Dynastic Houses

- No plan like yours to study history wisely.

Norman	Tudor
Plantagenet	Stuart
Lancaster	Hanover
York	Windsor

The Kings and Queens (Beginning with the House of Normandy)

- Willie, Willie, Harry, Stee,
  Harry, Dick, John, Harry Three,
  One, Two, Three Neds, Richard Two,
  Harry Four, Five, Six. Then who?
  Edward Four, Five, Dick the Bad,
  Harries twain and Ned the Lad,
  Mary, Bessie, James the Vain,
  Charlie, Charlie, James again.
  William and Mary, Anna Gloria,
  Four Georges, William and Victoria.
  Ned Seventh ruled till 1910,
  When George the Fifth came in, and then
  Ned Eight departed when love beckoned,
  Leaving George Six and Liz the Second.

William the Conqueror	Henry IV
William II	Henry V
Henry I	Henry VI
Stephen	Edward IV
Henry II	Edward V
Richard I	Richard III
John	Henry VII
Henry III	Henry VIII
Edward I	Edward VI
Edward II	Mary I
Edward III	Elizabeth I
Richard II	James I

Charles I	George IV
Charles II	William IV
James II	Victoria
William III and Mary II	Edward VII
Anne	George V
George I	Edward VIII
George II	George VI
George III	Elizabeth II

The Ranks of the Peerage (in Descending Order)

- **Do men ever visit Boston?**
- **Do men ever visit Britain?**

duke	viscount
marquis	baron
earl	

Great Fire of London: Year

- In sixteen hundred sixty-six London burned like rotten sticks.

English Reform Bill of 1832: Injustices Righted[47]

- **BURPS**

bribery	pocket boroughs
unrepresentative government	sale of seats
rotten boroughs	

Guy Fawkes Day

- Please to remember
  The fifth of November.
  Gunpowder, treason, and plot:
  This was the day the plot was contriv'd.
  To blow up the king and Parliament alive.

  Note: Guy Fawkes Day commemorates the 1605 Gunpowder Plot against James I and Parliament.

HORSE RACING

First Four Jockeys with More Than 6,000 Victories[48]

- **Long pink shoe cord**

Longden, Johnny	Shoemaker, Willie
Pincay, Laffit	Cordero, Angel

Horses That Have Won the Triple Crown (in Reverse Chronological Order)

- **A**fter **S**eattle **s**ecretary **c**ited **a**ssault, **c**ostly **w**orld **w**ar outweighed **Gal's** surgery.

HORSE	YEAR
Affirmed	1978
Seattle Slew	1977
Secretariat	1973
Citation	1948
Assault	1946
Count Fleet	1943
Whirlaway	1941
War Admiral	1937

Omaha	1935
Gallant Fox	1930
Sir Barton	1919

Note: The Triple Crown is won when the horse wins the Kentucky Derby, Belmont, and Preakness in the same year.

Horse Gaits

- **W**alking **g**als **t**rack **c**ars **p**retty **r**egularly.

walk	canter
gallop	pace
trot	run

HUNTING

A Rule for Shooting

- Never, never let your gun
  Pointed be at anyone.
  All the pheasants ever bred
  Won't make up for one man dead.

Steps in Firing a Rifle

- **BRASSF**

breathe	stop breathing
relax	squeeze slowly
aim	fire

LATIN

Common Verbs Governing the Dative Case[49]

- A Dative put, remember, pray,
  After envy, spare, obey
  Persuade, believe, command—to these
  Add pardon, succor, and displease.
  With *vacare*, to have leisure
  Add *placere*, to give pleasure.
  With *nubere*, of the female said:
  The English of it is "to wed."
  Servire add and add *studere*
  Favor, resist, and *indulgere*.

Latin Prepositions Taking the Ablative[50]

- *Ā*, *ab*, *absque*, *cōram*, *dē*,
  Palam, *cum*, and *ex*, or *e*.
  Sine, *tenus*, *prō*, and *prae*:
  Add *super*, *subter*, *sub*, and *in*,
  When "state," not "motion," 'tis they mean.

Latin Declension Rules[51]

- A Man, a name of People, and a Wind,
  River and Mountain, masculine we find:
  Romulus, Hispani, Zephyrus, Cocytus, Olympus.

  A Woman, Island, Country, Tree,
  and City, feminine we see:
  Penelope, Cyprus, Germania, Iaurus, Athenae.

To nouns that cannot be declined
the neuter gender is assigned:
Examples *fas* and *nefas* give
And the verb-noun infinitive:
Est summum nefas fallere:
Deceit is gross impiety.

Formation of Latin Verbs[52]

- He throws a fit
  Of righteous wrath,
  At *-BO, -BIS, -BIT*
  In 3rd or 4th.

  Present Subjunctives,
  I can't forget them.
  They're all *-AM,* except *AMO*
  And *AMO's AMEM.*

  Caesar was right, though rather cheeky,
  In saying, "*VENI, VIDI, VICI.*"
  Any boy is wrong who thinks he
  Said, "*VENIVI, VISI, VINXI.*"

Meanings of the Latin Stem *Malo*

- *Malo*—I would rather be
  Malo—in an apple tree
  Malo—than a wicked man
  Malo—in adversity."

LAW

Conditions for Valid Wills: New York and Some Other States

- A valid will must be **SWEPT**.

signed	published that it's a will
written	two witnesses' signatures
end signed	

Lemon Test

- **SEX**

  secular purpose
  effect must not advance or inhibit religion
  excessive state entanglement in religion prohibited

Note: The test comes from *Lemon v. Kurtzman*, 1971 and indicates the test the American government must satisfy to avoid violating the First Amendment's protection of religious freedom.

The 9 Felonies in Common Law

- **MR**. and **MRS**. **LAMB**

murder	larceny
rape	arson
manslaughter	mayhem
robbery	burglary
sodomy	

Adultery: Defenses

- **CRAP**

DEFENSE	EXPLANATION
condonation	The other party either explicitly forgave the adultery or at least slept with the adulterer after knowing about the adultery.
recrimination	Both are cheating.
act of adultery	Adultery doesn't automatically count in law, especially if it happened more than five years previously.
procurement or connivance of the other spouse	When adultery was the only ground for divorce in New York, some couples would cooperate in arranging that ground.

Divorce: Grounds in New York and Some Other States

- **A PAIN**

adultery
prison (imprisonment)
   for 3 years
abandonment

inhuman and cruel treatment
no-fault conversion divorce

Divorce: Factors for Determining Equal Distribution (Excludes Marital Property)

- **PAID SEAT**

property (separate)
age and health
income of each
duration of marriage

standard of living parties
earning capacity
any other relevant factor
tax

Slander vs. Libel

- Slander is said. Libel: pencil lead.

Search Warrant: Exceptions

- **COP IS ME.**

consent
open view
public place
incidental to a lawful
  arrest

stop and frisk a suspicious
  person
mobile premises
emergency

Hearsay Rule: Some Exceptions

- **SIR EAT DAMP**

state of mind of the
  speaker
impression
  (present sense
  impression)
record, business
excited testimony

dying declaration
against interest, declaration
miscellaneous
pedigree (statement of relationships)

LIBRARIES

The 10 Categories of the Dewey Decimal System

▪ Generally, philosophical religionists see language symbolically to favor literary history.

CATEGORY	CATALOG NUMBER
general works	000
philosophy and psychology	100
religion	200
social science	300
language	400
science (pure)	500
technology (useful arts, applied science)	600
fine arts	700
literature	800
history	900

Note: This system is the traditional method of categorizing books.

Order for Listing Basic Bibliographical Detail in Book Catalogs

▪ Fortunately, intelligent people prevent problems many pinheads fail to deflect.

frontispiece	maps
illustrations	plan
plates	facsimiles
photographs	tables
portraits	diagrams

LITERATURE: ANCIENT

Sophocles: Extant Plays

- **All airports ought to offer cooperation in ensuring peaceful travel.**

Ajax	*Ichneutai* (a satiric fragment)
Antigone	*Electra*
Oedipus Tyrannus	*Philoctetes*
Oedipus at Colonus	*Trachiniae*

Aristophanes: Extant Plays

- **Each person blames fortune to keep content.**

Ecclesiazusae	*Thesmophoriazusae*
Plutus	*The Knights*
The Birds	*The Clouds*
The Frogs	

MATH

ARITHMETIC AND PRE-ALGEBRA

Division: Procedures

- **Does** McDonald's serve cheeseburgers?
- **Does** my sister cook bananas?

divide   compare (remainder with
multiply   division)
subtract   bring down

Division: Rule for Checking

- **Ma** can help check your division.

multiply
add

Division: Determining the Divisibility of Numbers[53]

- Here are memory methods by which to decide,
  By glancing at numbers, the way they'll divide.
  When the unit is even, you quickly will see,
  The whole of the number by 2 cut can be.
  When the unit is either a naught or a 5,
  A slash with a 5 you throughout can contrive.

Any figures whatever you'll easily trace
By 2 and 5 cut, when beyond unit's place.
If the last two by 4 are divisible, see,
The whole line by 4 will divisible be.
When you find the last 3 can be cut by an 8,
8 will cut through them all, you may fearlessly state.
Cut the sum of the digits by 9 or by 3,
And in similar manner the number will be.
A number that's even, and by 3 divides,
Can always by 6 be divided besides.
When a number will cut up by 4 and 3, note,
It divides too by 12, you for certain can quote.
Whenever your digits alternately take,
And the sum of the series from the other will make,
11 or naught as a remainder, decide
You can by 11 that number divide.
It is only when 0 is the last figure seen,
That the series by 10 could divided have been.
For dividing by 7 no rule will apply,
If you doubt the assertion, to find a rule try.

If the last digit is even, the number is divisible by 2.
If the last digit is a 0 or a 5, the number is divisible by 5.
If the last two digits are divisible by 4, the number is
    divisible by 4.
If the last three digits are divisible by 8, then the number is
    divisible by 8.
If the sum of the digits is divisible by 9 or 3, then the
    number will be divisible by 9 or 3.
If the number is divisible by both 2 and 3, it is also divisible
    by 6.
If the number is divisible by both 3 and 4, it is also divisible
    by 12.
If you alternately add and subtract digits from left to
    right (thinking of the first digit as being added to zero),
    and the result is divisible by 11, the number is also
    divisible by 11.

Division: Definitions

- The divid**end** is on the **end** of a division problem.
- The quotien**t** is the resul**t**.

The three main terms in division are the *divisor* (the number that is being *divided into* a number), the *dividend* (the number that is being *divided by* a number), and the *quotient* (the result). For example, in 20 ÷ 10=2, the quotient is the result or 2, the dividend is the number being divided or 20, and the divisor is 10. In the fraction ½, the dividend is 1 (the numerator or top number) because it is the number that is being divided by another number (2); the divisor is 2 (the denominator or bottom number) because it is the number being divided into another number (1).

Division: Rule for Fractions

- The number you are dividing by
  Turn upside down and multiply.

- **K**entucky **c**hicken **f**ried
- **K**oalas **c**hasing **f**errets

  Keep the first fraction.
  Change the sign from divide to multiply.
  Flip the last fraction.

Fractions: Parts

- The **nu**merator is **u**p; the **d**enominator is **d**own.
- **N**otre **D**ame

  The *N* for numerator comes before (above) the *D* for denominator (below).

Fractions: Adding and Multiplying[54]

- You can add fractions that have the same bottom;
  Then, only the top numbers sum.
  You can multiply fractions any old time—
  Top times top and bottom times bottom.

In this mnemonic rhyme, the word *top* means the numerator, and the word *bottom* means the denominator. When you add fractions, you need the same denominator. If the denominators are not the same, you need to find the least common denominator. When you add fractions, make sure you add only the numerators because the denominators don't change. For example:

$$\frac{1}{5} + \frac{3}{5} = \frac{4}{5}$$

When multiplying fractions, it doesn't matter whether the denominators are the same, but you need to multiply the numerators together and the denominators together.

$$\frac{2}{7} \times \frac{2}{7} = \frac{2 \times 2}{7 \times 7} = \frac{4}{49}$$

To Find Percentages

- When *is* comes first
  Take the last into the first;
  When *is* comes last,
  Take the first into the last.

If asked, "Five is what percentage of 100?," divide 100 into 5. If asked, "What percentage of 100 is 5?," divide 100 into 5.

Multiplying: Two-Digit Numbers by Two-Digit Numbers

- Just ask **MOMA**.

  M = multiply   M = multiply
  O = write the 0   A = add

Multiplying: Rules for Positive and Negative Numbers

- If the signs match, that's a plus (+).
  If the signs clash, that's a bust (–).

- We win = good
- We lose = bad
- They win = bad
- They lose = good

positive × positive = positive
positive × negative = negative
negative × positive = negative
negative × negative = positive

The words *we* and *win* mean "positive," and the words *they* and *lose* mean "negative."

- If a good thing happens to a good person, that's good.
- If a good thing happens to a bad person, that's bad.
- If a bad thing happens to a good person, that's bad.
- If a bad thing happens to a bad person, that's good.

positive × positive = positive
positive × negative = negative
negative × positive = negative
negative × negative = positive

Multiplying a One-Digit Number by 9

- Turn both of your hands palms up. Begin with the finger farthest to the left (the thumb of your left hand) and count in the number of fingers you want to multiple by 9. Bend down that finger. The number of fingers to the left of the bent finger is the first digit of the product. The number of fingers to the right is the second digit of the product.

What is 5×9? Count in 5 fingers and bend that finger down (the pinky of your left hand). There are 4 fingers to the left and

5 fingers to the right; thus the product is 45 (5×9=45). What is 4×9? Count in 4 fingers and bend that finger down (the ring finger of your left hand). There are 3 fingers to the left and 6 fingers to the right; thus the product is 36 (4×9=36).

Greater Than and Less Than Symbols

- The alligator has to open its mouth wider for the larger number.

The angle of the symbol (> or <) is open close to the larger number or quantity and the vertex (point) of the angle is close to the smaller number or quantity.

Order of Operations

- **PEMDAS**
- **P**lease **e**xcuse **m**y **d**ear **a**unt **S**ally.
- **P**lease **e**ducate **m**y **d**aughters **a**nd **s**ons.

parentheses	multiplication and division
exponents	addition and subtraction

Commutative Property of Numbers

- The commuting distance is the same in each direction between home and work.

a+b=b+a
a×b=b×a

Associative Property of Numbers

- To associate with people is to group up with them.

(a+b)+c=a+(b+c)
(a×b)×c=a×(b×c)

Note: The associative property is about grouping.

Distributive Property of Numbers

- To distribute something is to give it to everyone.

  $a(b+c)=ab+ac$

  Note: The distributive property gives whatever is outside the parentheses to everything that's inside.

Metric Prefixes: From 10^3 to 10^{-3}

- **K**ing **H**ector's **d**affy **m**other **d**rinks **c**hocolate **m**ilk.
- **K**ing **H**enry **d**ied **M**onday **d**uring **C**hristmas **m**ass.

UNIT	SIZE
kilometer	10^3 or 1,000
hectometer	10^2 or 100
decameter	10^1 or 10
meter	1
decimeter	10^{-1} or $1/10$
centimeter	10^{-2} or $1/100$
millimeter	10^{-3} or $1/1000$

Note: This example uses meters, but the same prefixes are used for all metric units of measure.

Metric Prefixes: From 10^1 to 10^{12}

- **D**ecadent **H**ector **k**illed **M**eg's **g**igantic **t**errier.

PREFIX	SIZE
deca	10^1
hecto	10^2
kilo	10^3
mega	10^6
giga	10^9
tera	10^{12}

Metrix Prefixes: From 10^{-1} to 10^{-18}

- **D**arn **c**lever **m**nemonic **m**akes **n**o **p**refix **f**orgettable **abso**lutely.

PREFIX	SIZE
deci	10^{-1}
centi	10^{-2}
milli	10^{-3}
micro	10^{-6}
nano	10^{-9}
pic	10^{-12}
femto	10^{-15}
atto	10^{-18}

Roman Numerals

- Let **I** make one
  And **V** stand five,
  While **X** is ten,
  Then next arrive
  At **L** for fifty,
  But on we drive.
  C's a hundred.
  Followed by **D**
  (It's five hundred,
  Or you tell me).
  At last we come
  To **M**—a thousand
  A largish figure,
  You'll allow.

- **I** **v**iewed **X**erxes **l**oping **c**arelessly **d**own **m**ountains.

I = 1	C = 100
V = 5	D = 500
X = 10	M = 1,000
L = 50	

Note: To multiply the value of any Roman numeral by 1,000 simply put a horizontal bar over it. Thus $\overline{M}$ equals $1,000 \times 1,000$ or $1,000,000$.

MEASURES OF CENTRAL TENDENCY

Mode

- **Mo**de is the value occurring **mo**st of the time.

  Example: In the set 2, 4, 7, 2, 8, the number 2 is the mode.

Median

- The me**d**ian is the number in the mi**dd**le of the data.
- The median splits the data down the middle, like the median strip in a road.

  Example: In the set 3, 4, 5, the number 4 is the median.

  Note: The median is the number in the middle of the data set when the values are ordered from the least to the greatest. If there is an odd number of values in the set, the median is the value in the middle. If there is an even number of values in the set, the median is the average of the two middle numbers.

Mean

- Calling someone average can be mean.

  Note: The mean of a data set is the average of the values, determined by adding up all the values and then dividing the sum by the number of items in the set. For example, the mean of the values 30, 40, 50, $60 = (30+40+50+60) \div 4 = 180 \div 4 = 45$.

Adding: Positive and Negative Numbers

- **GADS** = **G**reater **a**bsolute value **d**ecides **s**ign.

Note: The absolute value of a number is the distance from zero to that number on the number line. When you add two numbers with absolute signs, find the difference of their absolute values. Using GADS, the sum should get the sign with the greater absolute value. For example, what is $-8+5$? First, find the absolute value of each integer: For -8, the absolute value $=8$; for $+5$, the absolute value is 5. The number 8 has the largest absolute value, so the sum will be negative. Next, find the difference between 8 and 5 ($8-5=3$). Therefore the answer is -3.

Scientific Notation

- Positive power requires moving in the right direction.
- Negative power requires moving into left field.

Note: Scientific notation enables us to write extremely large or small numbers in an abbreviated form. When a number is written in scientific notation, and you want to write its value in standard notation, you move the decimal point to either the right or the left, depending on whether the exponent is positive or negative. The exponent tells you the number of spaces to move the decimal point. Using the mnemonic devices, write 2×10^6 and 4×10^{-6} in standard notation. When the power is positive, move decimal point the indicated places to the right. Thus $2 \times 10^6 = 2,000,000$. When the power is negative, move the decimal point the indicated places to the left. Thus $4 \times 10^{-6} = .000004$.

Negative Exponents[55]

- The exhausted swimmer had negative power going into the last flip-turn.

When dealing with negative exponents, flip the fraction over and change the sign to positive.

Note: Competitive swimmers use a flip-turn to change direction quickly when they reach the end of a pool. The term *flip-turn* will remind you to flip the fraction and the sign. For example, $X^{-2} = \dfrac{X^{-2}}{1}$; flip the fraction and change the sign to get $\dfrac{1}{X^2}$. For example, $3^{-3} = \dfrac{3^{-3}}{1} = \dfrac{1}{3^3} = \dfrac{1}{3 \times 3 \times 3} = \dfrac{1}{27}$.

Raising a Base to a Zero Power

- Raising a nonzero number to the zero power is easily done because the result is always one.

Note: Raising any nonzero number to the power of zero yields the number 1. You can see that operation will yield the number 1 if you realize what happens when you divide two powers with the same base. For example, $\dfrac{X^6}{X^2} = X^{6-2} = X^4$. Assume now that the exponential expression in the numerator is equal to the expression in the denominator, say $\dfrac{X^6}{X^6}$. You know that a (nonzero) number divided by itself equals 1. You also know that when you simplify $\dfrac{X^6}{X^6}$, you subtract, giving you X^{6-6} or X^0; $X^0 = 1$. In other words, 10^0, 5^0, and 6^0 all equal 1.

SQUARE ROOTS

In these mnemonic devices, the number of letters in each word represents the digits.

Square Root of 2 (to 3 Decimal Places)

- I wish I knew (the root of 2).
- I want a duet.

1.414

Square Root of 2 (to 10 Decimal Places)[56]

▪ I have a root of a two whose square is two.

1.4142135623

Square root of 3 (to 3 Decimal Places)

▪ O charmed was he (to know the root of 3).

1.732

Square Root of 5 (to 3 Decimal Places)

▪ So we now strive (to know the root of 5).

2.236

Square Root of 6 (to 3 Decimal Places)

▪ We know your hexagrams.

2.449

Square Root of 7 (to 3 Decimal Places)

▪ We recall root seven.

2.645

Square root of 8 (to 3 Decimal Places)

▪ We determine by octagons.

2.828

Cups, Pints, Quarts, and Gallons

- A **cup** is one half **pint**, which is one half **quart**, which is a quarter of a **gallon**, which is four quarts.

  The length of each word reveals the measure's relative size.

The Number of Feet in a Mile

- Five tomatoes: 5 2 8 0

  5,280 feet

ALGEBRA

Multiplying Binomials

- **FOIL**

  first terms   inside terms
  outside terms   last terms

  Note: What is $(x+2)(x+3)$? Multiply the *first terms* in the binomials: $x \times x = x^2$. Multiply the *outside terms* (the first term of the first binomial by the second term in the second binomial): $x \times 3 = 3x$. Multiply the *inside terms* (the second term of the first binomial by the first term of the second binomial): $2 \times x = 2x$. Multiply the *last terms* in the binomials: $2 \times 3 = 6$. Finally, add the results, combining like terms: $x^2 + 3x + 2x + 6 = x^2 + 5x + 6$.

Coordinate Plane: Numbering of the Quadrants[57]

- The coordinate plane writes a C.

  If an airplane starts in quadrant I and flies through the remaining quadrants in order, it will create the letter *C*.

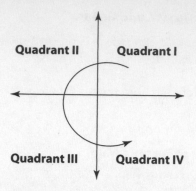

Quadrant II | Quadrant I

Quadrant III | Quadrant IV

Note: The coordinate plane is the two-dimensional plane containing the *x*- and *y*-axes. The axes divide the coordinate plane into four regions or quadrants.

Coordinate Plane: Positive or Negative by Quadrant

- **BYNX**

both *x* and *y* are positive in quadrant I
y is positive in quadrant II
neither is positive in quadrant III
x is positive in quadrant IV

Coordinate Pair: Plotting[58]

- *X* before *Y*, walk before you fly.
- *Y*-sie rise-y; *X* a-cross.

In a coordinate pair the *x* (horizontal axis) comes first and the *y* (vertical axis) comes second.

Formula for Financial Interest

- I am pretty: I = prt.

  interest   rate
  principal   time

  Note: Interest = principal × rate × time.

Formula for Distance

- **DiRT**

  distance
  rate
  time

  Note: Distance = rate × time.

Elements of the Matrix

The determinant of this matrix is used in the conic sections part of analytic geometry.

- **A**ll **h**airy **g**orillas **h**ave **b**ig **f**eet **g**ood **f**or **c**limbing.
- **A**ll **h**appy **g**irls **h**aving **b**oyfriends **g**o **f**or **c**inema.

$$\begin{bmatrix} a & h & g \\ h & b & f \\ g & f & c \end{bmatrix}$$

Parallel and Perpendicular Lines: Definitions[59]

- para ↕↕ el
- pErpEndicular

Parallel lines are lines that never intersect. Perpendicular lines intersect to form a 90° angle.

Note: Think of the two *L*s in *parallel* as parallel lines. Remember that the two *E*s in *perpendicular* each contain 3 horizontal lines that are perpendicular to the vertical line of the letter.

Right Angle[60]

- The **right** way to sit is with your back straight in the chair.

When you sit properly in a chair, your back and lap (or the seat of the chair) meet at a 90°, or right, angle.

Complementary vs. Supplementary Angles

- *S* is made with two *C*s.
- *C* comes before *S* in the alphabet.

Supplementary angles (which total 180°) are twice the size of complementary angles (which total 90°).
Complementary angles are smaller (and hence come before) than supplementary angles.

Triangles: Equilateral, Isosceles, and Scalene[61]

- **Equi**lateral triangles have three sides of **equ**al length; the letter **E** has 3 bars.
- **I**sosceles triangles have two equal or congruent sides, like the top and bottom bars of the letter **I**.
- **S**calene triangles have no congruent sides, like the letter **S**.

Triangles: Isosceles

- Oh isosceles, oh isosceles . . .
  Two angles have
  Equal degrees

  Oh isosceles, oh isosceles . . .
  Two sides alike
  Just like my knees.

Oh isosceles, oh isosceles . . .
You look just like
A Christmas tree.

Right Triangle: Hypotenuse

- *Hypotenuse* is a long word, and it describes the longest part of a right triangle.

Pythagorean Theorem

- The squaw on the hippopotamus is equal to the sum of the squaws on the other two hides.

$$\text{Hypotenuse}^2 = \text{base}^2 + \text{height}^2$$

Note: This mnemonic device is the punch line of an old joke that begins like this: there were three Indians who met to trade wives. The first Indian told his wife to sit on a blanket made from the skin of a deer, the second Indian placed his wife on a hide made of buffalo . . . The hypotenuse is the side opposite the 90° angle in a right triangle. The Pythagorean theorem enables one to find the length of any side given the lengths of the other two sides.

Pentagon: Area

- O! Eustace is **a square**.

$A = 1.72a^2$, where a = length of one side.

Note: The number of letters in the first three words of the mnemonic represents the number in the formula. The first exclamation point is the decimal, and the five words represents the pentagon.

Circle: Area

- **A**pple **p**ies **are square**.
- **A**pple **p**ies **are r**ound.

$A = \text{pi} \times \text{radius}^2$ (or pi $\times$ radius $\times$ radius)

Circle: Circumference

- Cherry **p**ie **d**elicious!

  $C = \text{pi} \times \text{diameter}$

Pi (π)

Pi (the ratio of the circumference to the diameter of a circle) is an irrational number and thus cannot be written with decimals that end or repeat. Mnemonic devices in which the number of letters in each word represents a digit in the value of pi are used to help people memorize the value of pi (3.14159265358979323 8462643383279 . . .) to many digits.

Pi to 7 Places

- How I wish I could calculate pi!

  3.141592

Pi to 8 Places

- May I have a large container of coffee?

  3.145926

Pi to 15 Places[62]

- Now, Dot, I find I still determine to suffer fools who laugh whenever Grandpapa insults Grandmama.
- How I want a drink, alcoholic of course, after the heavy chapters involving quantum mechanics.

  3.14159265358979 (in the first device case, *Dot*=the decimal point).

Pi to 21 Places

- Sir, I send a rhyme excelling in sacred truth and rigid spelling; numerical sprites elucidate for me the Lexicon's dull weight.

3.14159265358979323846

Pi to 31 Places[63]

- Now I will a rhyme construct,
  By chosen words the young instruct,
  Cunningly devised endeavor.
  Con it and remember ever
  Widths in circle here you see
  Sketched out in strange obscurity.

3.1415926535897932384626433383279

Note: There are contests for people who, through the use of such mnemonic systems, are capable of memorizing the value of pi to thousands of digits. On October 3–4, 2006, Akira Haraguchi, a Japanese mental-health worker, recited 100,000 digits of pi. It took him more than 16 hours.

TRIGONOMETRY

Triangles: Length of the Sides

- **SOH-CAH-TOA**
- **S**ome **o**ld **h**orses **c**an **a**lways **h**ear **t**heir **o**wner's **a**pproach.
- **O**scar/**h**ad **a**/**h**airy **o**ld/**a**rmpit.

S=sine	C=cosine
O=opposite side	A=adjacent side
H=hypotenuse	T=tangent

Note: If you know one side of a right triangle and the measure of an angle besides the right angle, you can determine the lengths of the other two sides using trigonometric ratios. Sine equals the opposite side over (divided by) the hypotenuse; cosine equals the adjacent side over the hypotenuse; tangent equals the opposite side over the adjacent side:

$$\text{sine} = \frac{\text{opposite}}{\text{hypotenuse}}, \text{cosine} = \frac{\text{adjacent}}{\text{hypotenuse}}, \text{and tangent} = \frac{\text{opposite}}{\text{adjacent}}$$

Positive Functions in Each Quadrant

- **A**ll **s**tudents **t**ake **c**alculus.

  all trig ratios in quadrant I
  sine ratios in quadrant II
  tangent ratios in quadrant III
  cosine ratios in quadrant IV

Euler's Constant

In these mnemonic devices, the number of letters in each word represents a different digit in the constant *e* to 10 decimal places.

- To express *e* remember to memorize a sentence to simply this!
- We require a mnemonic to remember *e* whenever we scribble math.

  2.7182818284

- 2.7—Andrew Jackson—Andrew Jackson—Isosceles Right Triangle

Andrew Jackson, who served 2 terms, was elected the 7th president of the United States in 1828. The three angles of an isosceles right triangle are 45, 90, and 45. The mnemonic works out to 15 places: $e = 2.718281828459045$.

Note: Euler's constant is the base of Napierian, or natural, logarithms.

CALCULUS

Order of Taking the Derivative of a Quotient

- hi-di-hi, hi-di-ho, ho-ho

  ho = bottom
  hi = top
  di = derivative

  Note that $\dfrac{d}{dx}\dfrac{\text{hi}}{\text{ho}} = \dfrac{\text{ho} \times \text{hi}' - \text{hi} \times \text{ho}'}{\text{ho}^2}$.

MEDICINE, ANATOMY, AND PHYSIOLOGY

Treating Patients with Red and Pale Faces

- When the face is red, raise the head.
  When the face is pale, raise the tail.

First Aid: Noncorrosive Poison

- **FDR**

  fill = give liquid to victim
  drain = induce vomiting
  refill = introduce more liquid into victim

First Aid: Restoring Breathing

- A quick check

  airway=open passage
  quick breaths=provide two breaths for adults or four puffs
  for children
  check=breathing, pulse, spontaneous recovery, and general
  appearance

Properties of Bile

- Bile from the liver emulsifies greases
  Tinges the urine and colors the feces
  Aids peristalsis, prevents putrefaction
  If you remember all this, you'll give satisfaction.

Functions of Blood

- **O**ld **C**harlie **F**oster **h**ates **w**omen **h**aving **d**ull **c**lothes.

  oxygen transport   waste
  carbon dioxide transport hormones
  food   disease
  heat   clotting

Blood Donors and Receivers

- **D**onors give. To **ab**ate is to take away.

  People with type O blood can donate blood to anyone
  (universal donors).
  People with type AB blood can receive blood from anyone
  (universal recipients).

How the Heart Works[64]

- The chambers on the right
  Are busy pumping blood.

The chambers on the right
Pump blood to the lungs.
The carbon dioxide
In the blood is removed.
That's how the heart works out!

The chambers on the left
Are busy pumping blood.
The chambers on the left
Pump blood from the lungs.
They pump it to the body
With fresh oxygen.
That's how the heart works out!

The chambers on the left,
The chambers on the right,
The chambers of the heart
Pump blood day and night.
The atria and ventricles
Are pumping blood about.
That's how the heart works out!

Note: Sing to the tune of "The Hokey Pokey."

The 6 Most Common Elements in the Human Body (in Decreasing Order)

- **O**scar **c**arried **H**enry's **n**ice **c**alf **p**hysically.

oxygen	nitrogen
carbon	calcium
hydrogen	phosphorous

The 5 Heaviest Human Organs

- **S**kip **l**ifted **B**rian's **l**aw book **h**eartily.

skin	lungs
liver	heart
brain	

Systems of the Human Body[65]

- The human body is made of a lot.
  It runs on the many systems it's got.

  The skeletal system consists of bones.
  It forms a framework hard as stones.

  The muscular system helps us to move.
  Muscles allow our strength to improve.

  The digestive system breaks down our food.
  The stomach goes to work once the mouth has chewed.

  The respiratory system lets us breathe.
  Our lungs take in air, then let it leave.

  The circulatory system carries our blood.
  The heart, veins, and arteries handle the flood.

  The excretory system removes our waste.
  Our kidneys and colon make sure it's erased.

  The reproductive system creates our young.
  Giving parents a daughter or son.

  The endocrine system consists of glands.
  They help us cope with our growth demands.

  The nervous system controls how we act.
  Our brain and spinal cord keep behavior intact.

  The immune system protects us from disease.
  Our skin blocks germs from a cough or sneeze.

  The human body is made of a lot.
  It runs on the many systems it's got.

  Note: Sing to the tune of "Hush, Little Baby."

Skeletal System[66]

- There are bones in our body,
  The skeletal system.
  There are bones in our body,
  Over two hundred bones.

  The cranium's the skull bone.
  The hammer's the ear bone.
  The nasal's the nose bone.
  We have many bones.

  The maxilla's the upper jaw.
  The mandible's the lower jaw.
  The zygoma's the cheekbone.
  We have many bones.

  The frontal's the forehead.
  The clavicle's the collarbone.
  The scapula's the shoulder blade.
  We have many bones.

  The sternum's the breastbone.
  The vertebrae are spine bones.
  The innominate's the hip bone.
  We have many bones.

  The femur's the thighbone.
  The tibia's the shinbone.
  The fibula's the calf bone.
  We have many bones.

  The humerus is the upper arm.
  The radius is the main forearm.
  The patella's the kneecap.
  We have many bones.

  The carpal's the wrist bone.
  Metacarpals are hand bones.

Phalanges are finger bones.
We have many bones.

The tarsus are ankle bones.
Metatarsals are foot bones.
Phalanges are toe bones.
We have many bones.

There are bones in our body,
The skeletal system.
There are bones in our body,
Over two hundred bones.

Note: Sing to the tune of "There's a Hole in the Bucket."

Number of Sets of Chromosomes: Diploid vs. Haploid Cells[67]

- haploid vs. diploid

The word *haploid* has one *I* for one set of chromosomes; the word *diploid* has two *I*s for two sets of chromosomes.

Note: Fungus is usually a haploid organism, and gametes (sperm and egg cells) are haploid. A diploid cell has two sets of each chromosome. Most animal cells are diploid.

The Excretory Organs of the Body

- **SKILL**

skin	liver
kidneys	lungs
intestines	

Number of Bones in Adult Human

- Hbones=6

  B=2 (2nd letter in device and 2nd letter in alphabet)
  O=0
  6=6 (number of letters in *Hbones*)

  Note: Adult human beings have 206 bones.

The 4 Largest Human Bones

- Fester told fibs humorously.

femur	fibula
tibia	humerus

Bones of the Skull

- Old people from Texas eat spiders.

occipital	temporal
parietal	ethmoid
frontal	sphenoid

Human Bones from Shoulder Blade to Fingers

- Some criminals have underestimated Royal Canadian Mounted Police.

scapula (shoulder blade)	radius (forearm)
clavicle (collarbone)	carpals (wrist)
humerus (upper arm)	metacarpals (palm)
ulna (forearm)	phalanges (fingers)

The Carpal Bones

- Sue likes Terry's pens; her cap's too tight.

scaphoid

lunate

triquetral

pisiform

hamate

capitate

trapezoid

trapezium

Human Bones from the Hip to the Toes

- Help from police to find the missing prisoner.

hip

femur (thigh)

patella (kneecap)

tibia (lower leg)

fibula (lower leg)

tarsals (ankle)

metatarsals (foot)

phalanges (toes)

Nerves through the Superior Orbital Tissue (in Order)

- Large feathers tickle leprechauns naked in America.

lacrimal

frontal

trochlear

lateral

nasociliary

internal

abducent

The 5 Layers of the Scalp

- SCALP

skin

connective tissue

aponeurosis

loose connective tissue

periosteum

Superficial Branches of the Facial Nerve

- Teddy Zucker's bowels move constantly.

temporal
zygomatic
buccal

mandibular
cervical

The 4 Parasympathetic Ganglia

- COPS

ciliary
otic

pterygopalatine
submandibular

Important Structures in the Costal Groove (in Order Going Interiorly)

- VAN

vein
artery
nerve

Characteristics of the Spleen

- 1, 3, 5, 7, 9, 11

1 inch by 3 inches by 5 inches in size
7 ounces in weigh
lies obliquely between the 9th and 11th ribs

Sections of the Intestinal Track (in Order)

- Dow Jones Industrial averages closing stock report.

duodenum
jejunum
ileum
appendix

colon
sigmoid colon
rectum

Path of the Facial Nerve in the Facial Canal

- **O**scar **be**haved **d**readfully.

    outward
    backward
    downward

Cranial Nerves

- **O**nce **O**pie **o**gled **t**he **t**eacher **an**d **f**aced **v**ery **g**rave **v**itupera-tion **an**d **h**ysteria.

    olfactory   facial
    optic   vestibulocochlear (acoustic)
    oculomotor   glossopharyngeal
    trochlear   vagus
    trigeminal   auditory, spinal
    abducens   hypoglossal

Nerves Entering the Hand (Anterior Surface of the Wrist)

- **RUM**

    radial
    ulnar
    median

Clinical Manifestation of Injury to the Radial, Ulnar, and Median Nerves

- **W**ind **c**lock **t**oday.

    wrist drop
    claw hand
    tunnel syndrome

Location of Blood Vessels in Hip (in Order from Outside to Inside)

- **NAVY**

  nerve   vein
  artery   Y represents the crotch

Physician's Orders When Admitting a Patient to the Hospital

- **D. C. VAN DISSEL**

  diagnosis   intake and output
  condition   symptomatic drug
  vital signs   specific drugs
  ambulation   examinations
  nursing order   laboratory
  diet

5 Drugs That Can Be Placed in an Endotracheal Tube

- **ALIEN**

  atropine   epinephrine
  lidocaine   Narcan
  isuprel

Factors in Evaluating Patients

- **SOAP**

  subjective   assessment
  objective   plan

Diet for Diarrhea

- **BRAT**

  bananas   apples
  rice   toast

Causes of Diseases

- **VITAMIN C DIP**

vascular	neoplastic
infective	congenital
trauma	degenerative
allergy/immunological	idiopathic
metabolic/endocrine	psychogenic
iatrogenic	

Wounds: 4 Types

- **CLIP**

crush	incision
laceration	puncture

Wounds: 5 Types

- **A PAIL**

abrasion	incision
puncture	laceration
avulsion	

Causes of Abnormal Gait

- **A**ll **p**atients **s**pending **c**ash **s**ee **p**roper **d**octors.

apraxia or ataxia	sensory deficit
parkinsonism	proximal myopathy
spasticity	distal myopathy
cerebellar ataxia	

Factors Causing Back Pain

- **O, VESALIUS**

  osteomyelitis

  vertebral fracture

  extraspinal tumors

  spondylolisthesis

  ankylosing spondylitis

  lumbar disk disease

  intraspinal tumors

  unhappiness

  stress

Note: This mnemonic comes from the name of the Flemish anatomist who was among the first to describe the spine in detail.

Signs of Cerebellar Dysfunction

- **DANISH**

  dysdiadochokinesia

  ataxia

  nystagmus

  intention tremor

  speech problems

  hypotonia

Symptoms of Gerstmann Syndrome

- **A-ALF**

  agraphia

  acalculia

  left/right disorientation

  finger agnosia

Note: This syndrome is a congenital disorder.

Basic Somatotypes (Body Types)[68]

- **End**omorphs have big **end**s.

  They're soft and round.

- **M**esomorphs are **m**uscular.

  They're hard, muscular, and athletic-looking.

- **Ec**tomorphs are **t**hin.

  They're skinny.

MILITARY

Army Ranks[69]

- **P**rivates **c**an't **s**alute **w**ithout **l**earning **c**orrect **m**ilitary command grades.

private	captain
corporal	major
sergeant	colonel
warrant officer	general
lieutenant	

Ranks of Generals

- **B**e **m**y **l**ittle **g**eneral.

brigadier (1 star)	lieutenant (3 stars)
major (2 stars)	general (4 stars)

Marine Corps: Basic Principles of War

- **MOOSE-MUSS**

mass	movement
objective	unity of command
offensive	simplicity
surprise	security
economy of offense	

Marine Corps: Guidelines for Machine Gun Emplacement

- **COCOA**

cover	obstacles
observation	avenues of approach
concealment	

Marine Corps: Five-Paragraph Tactical Order

- **SMEAC**

station	administration
mission	command and control and
execution	logistics

Marine Island-Hopping Campaign in the Pacific: World War II[70]

- **BIGOT**

Bougainville	Okinawa
Iwo Jima	Tarawa
Guadalcanal	

U.S. Army: Procedures to Orient the Firing of Artillery Pieces

- Take the **fire** out of the **o**ld **l**ady.

  Take the azimuth of **fire** out of the **o**rienting **l**ine.

U.S. Army: Factors to Consider When Planning a Tactical Operation

- **METT**

mission	troop
enemy	terrain

Primary Types of National Defense

- **NBC**

nuclear
biological
chemical

MORSE CODE

To remember the combinations of dots and dashes symbolizing the letters used in Morse code, use the following mnemonic, where short syllables signify dots and long syllables signify dashes.[71]

LETTER	MORSE CODE	MNEMONIC
A	. -	alone
B	- . . .	beautifully
C	- . - .	come a cropper
D	- . .	daintily
E	.	egg
F	. . - .	for a fortnight
G	- - .	good gracious
H	. . . .	ha ha ha ha
I	. .	Is it?
J	. - - -	Japan's jam jars
K	- . -	kiss me Kate

L	. - . .	linoleum
M	- -	my mate
N	- .	naughty
O	- - -	our old oak
P	. - - .	polite person
Q	- - . -	quite queer and quaint
R	. - .	rewarding
S	. . .	sh sh sh
T	-	tea
U	. . -	underneath
V	. . . -	very verbose
W	. - -	without waste
X	- . . -	extra expense
Y	- . - -	yellow yacht's yarn
Z	- - . .	zoologic

LETTER	MORSE CODE	MNEMONIC
A	. -	a-BOUT
B	- . . .	BOIS-ter-ous-ly
C	- . - .	CARE less CHILD-ren
D	- . .	DAN-ger-ous
E	.	eh?
F	. . - .	fe-ne-STRA-tion
G	- - .	GOOD GRA-vy!
H	. . . .	hee hee hee hee
I	. .	aye aye
J	. - - -	ju-LY'S JANE JONES!
K	- . -	KET-tle KORN
L	. - . .	li-NO-le-um
M	- -	MORE MILK!
N	- .	NA-vy
O	- - -	OH! MY! GOD!
P	. - - .	pa-RADE PAN-el
Q	- - . -	QUEEN'S WED-ding DAY
R	. - .	ro-TA-tion
S	. . .	si si si
T	-	THRUST

LETTER	MORSE CODE	MNEMONIC
U	. . -	un-der WHERE?!
V	. . . -	va-va-va-VOOM!
W	. - -	with WHITE WHALE
X	- . . -	EX-tra ex-PENSE
Y	- . - -	YEL-low YO-YO
Z	- - . .	ZINC ZOO-keep-er

MOVIES

James Bond Films with Sean Connery

The first five James Bond films (all with Sean Connery) are in alphabetical order:

- D F G T Y

MOVIE	YEAR
Dr. No	1962
From Russia with Love	1963
Goldfinger	1964
Thunderball	1965
You Only Live Twice	1967

Note: Connery came back to act in *Diamonds Are Forever* (1971) and *Never Say Never Again* (1983), a rescripted version of *Thunderball*.

Marx Brothers' Movies[72]

- Could any movie house deny one really rare clip with star comedians laughing?

MOVIE	YEAR
Cocoanuts	1929
Animal Crackers	1930
Monkey Business	1931
Horse Feathers	1932
Duck Soup	1933
A Night at the Opera	1935
A Day at the Races	1937
Room Service	1938
At the Circus	1939
Go West	1940
The Big Store	1941
A Night in Casablanca	1946
Love Happy	1949

Note: There are several mnemonics for remembering the 13 Marx Brothers' movies in sequence. Movies 2–5 each have an animal in the title. The first letter of the middle five (when key letters are removed), spell DORRC.

Oscar-Winning Best Films (2000–2005)

- Gladiator—Mind
  Chicago—Lord
  Million Dollar—**Crash**

MOVIE	YEAR
Gladiator	2000
A Beautiful Mind	2001
Chicago	2002
The Lord of the Rings:	
The Return of the King	2003
Million Dollar Baby	2004
Crash	2005

MUSIC

Notes of the Treble Clef Lines

- Every good boy does fine.
- Every good boy deserves fudge. (My favorite!)
- Empty garbage before Dad flips.
- Elephants go belly dancing Fridays.

E
G
B
D
F

Notes of the Bass Clef Spaces

- All cows eat grass.
- All cars eat gas.
- All Cajuns eat gumbo.
- All cats eat goldfish.

A
C
E
G

Notes of the Bass Clef Lines

- Girls buy dolls for amusement.
- Good boys deserve fun always.
- Good boys do fine always.

- Grizzly bears don't fly airplanes.
- Go beyond doors for answers.

G

B

D

F

A

Note: The last device is courtesy of my friend Justin Gruver.

Order of Sharps for Sharp Key Signatures

- Father Charles goes down and ends battle.
- Frédéric Chopin goes down and ends battle.
- Five cats got drowned at east Boston.
- Fat cats go down alleys eating birds.
- Fidel Castro got drunk after every battle.

F

C

G

D

A

E

B

Order of Flats for Flat Key Signatures

- Blanket exploded and Daddy got cold feet.
- Be exciting and daring, go climb fences.
- Buy eight apple donuts, get coffee free.
- Big elephants at dinner gobble curly fries.

B

E

A

D

G

C

F

Notes of the 6 Guitar Strings (from Lowest to Highest)

- Even after dinner giraffes bend easily.
- Every American dog goes ballistic eventually.
- Every American dad goes bald eventually.
- Eddie ate dynamite. Good-bye Eddie.

E
A
D
G
B
E

Order of Musical Modes

The musical modes are based on the white keys of a piano starting with C.

- I don't play loud music after lectures.
- I don't particularly like modes a lot.
- I don't particularly like my appendix licked.
- I don't play like mariachis after lunch.
- I don't pretend Lydia makes any logic.

Ionian mode	Mixolydian mode
Dorian mode	Aeolian mode
Phrygian mode	Locrian mode
Lydian mode	

Four Sections of a Symphony Orchestra

- Sinners will be punished.

string	brass
woodwind	percussion

Major Composers of the Classical Period (c. 1750–c. 1820)

- Glorious bells have many beautiful sounds.

Gluck	Mozart, W. A.
Bach, C. P. E.	Beethoven
Haydn	Schubert

Major Composers of the Romantic Period (c. 1810–c. 1910)

- Some boors making caustic statements love wasting very big moments to mouth depressing sarcasm.

Schubert	Verdi
Berlioz	Brahms
Mendelssohn	Mussorgsky
Chopin	Tchaikovsky
Schumann	Mahler
Liszt	Debussy
Wagner	Strauss, Richard

Gilbert or Sullivan?

- In the alphabet,
  G comes before *S*,
  L before *M*.
  So Gilbert wrote the lyrics,
  Sullivan the music.

Note: Gilbert and Sullivan were an operatic team.

MYTHOLOGY

Greek: 9 Muses

- Can Carl educate Tom's mother to empty Pop's urn?

NAME	PRESIDED OVER	ADDITIONAL MNEMONIC
Calliope	epic poetry	name contains the letters that spell *epic*
Clio	history	both words have the same two vowels
Erato	erotic or love poetry and song	remember *erotic*
Thalia	comedy	name has an *H* for "humor," contains *ha*
Melpomene	tragedy	name contains *elp*
Terpsichore	dancing	"trips" while dancing; name contains *choir*
Euterpe	lyric poetry	name contains *ute*; she was depicted holding a flute
Polyhymnia	sacred poetry and song	name contains *hymn*
Urania	astronomy	remember the planet

Note: The Greek Muses were daughters of Zeus and Mnemosyne and presided over learning and the arts.

Greek: Gods[73]

- Poseidon was god of the ocean
  And Ares was god over war.
  Athena was goddess of wisdom.
  These gods ancient Greeks did adore.
  Chorus
  Greek gods, Greek gods,
  The rulers in old Greek mythology,
  Greek gods, Greek gods,
  The rulers in mythology.

  Artemis was goddess of hunting.
  Apollo was god over light
  And Hermes protected all travelers.
  Each god possessed powerful might.
  [Chorus]
  Hypnos was god over sleeping
  And Eros was god over love.
  The goddess of marriage was Hera,
  Upon Mount Olympus above.
  [Chorus]
  The goddess of plants was Demeter.
  The god of the forest was Pan.
  The love goddess was Aphrodite.
  The spreading of love was her plan.
  [Chorus]
  The underworld ruler was Hades.
  The ruler of all gods was Zeus.
  Adored by the ancient Greek people
  From Athens to old Syracuse.
  [Chorus]

  Note: Sing to the tune of "My Bonnie Lies over the Ocean."

Roman: Gods[74]

- Cupid was the god of love
  In Roman mythology.

Neptune was the god of the sea
In Roman mythology.

Venus was the goddess of love
In Roman mythology.
Mars was the god of war
In Roman mythology.
Chorus
How they ruled, how they ruled,
How they ruled so powerfully!
On the hills of Rome
Gods made their home
In Roman mythology.

Vulcan was the god of fire
In Roman mythology.
Diana was the goddess of the moon
In Roman mythology.

Somnus was the god of sleep
In Roman mythology.
Juno was the queen of the gods
In Roman mythology.
[Chorus]
Janus guarded doors and gates
In Roman mythology.
Mercury protected travelers
In Roman mythology.

Minerva was the goddess of wisdom
In Roman mythology.
Ceres was the goddess of growth
In Roman mythology.
[Chorus]
Apollo was the god of light
In Roman mythology.
Saturn was the god of crops
In Roman mythology.

Pluto ruled the underworld
In Roman mythology.
And Jupiter ruled over all the gods
In Roman mythology.
[Chorus]

Note: Sing to the tune of "Polly Wolly Doodle."

NAUTICAL NAVIGATION

Port vs. Starboard

- Port=left; they have the same number of letters.
- Starboard=right; the word has two *R*s.
- Remember the *R*s in *starboard*, and you'll be right as rain.

Running Lights on Naval Vessels

- Red Port wine

  Red is on the port side, and thus green is on the starboard.

- Red right returning

  When returning from sea the red markers should be on your right (or starboard) side, and the green markers should be on your left (or port) side.

Marine Traffic Rules

- When all three I see ahead,
  I turn to Starboard and show my Red;
  Green to Green, Red to Red,
  Perfect safety—Go Ahead.

But if to Starboard Red appear,
It is my duty to keep clear—
To act as judgment says is proper;
To Port or Starboard, Back or Stop her.

And if upon my Port is seen
A steamer's Starboard light of Green,
I hold my course and watch to see
That Green to Port keeps Clear of me.

Both in safety and in doubt
Always keep a good look out.
In Danger, with no room to turn,
Ease her, Stop her, Go Astern.

How to Pass a Boat

- Green to green or red to red,
  Perfect safety, go ahead.
  Red to green or green to red,
  Drop the anchor, collision ahead.

The Depth of a Fathom

- Six letters, six feet

Note: Mark Twain took his pen name from the name of two fathoms (twain), the minimum navigable depth of the Mississippi River, along which he piloted as a riverboat driver.

Buoyage

- **Even red** nuns have **odd green** cans.

  Tapered red buoys are even numbered.
  Cylindrical green buoys are odd numbered.

Note: The word *nuns* in this context describes cone-shaped buoys.

Buoyage: Numbering

- **DEMODS:** Buoy numbers **de**crease **mo**ving **d**ownstream.

Boating Advice: Etiquette and Safety[75]

- **G**enerally, **a**nchoring **o**ur **r**ed **t**ugboat **d**iligently **m**inimizes **s**urge **l**oads.

General responsibility: Above all else, avoid a collision, regardless of whether you have right of way.

Anchored, stopped, or moored boats must be avoided by all other vessels.

Overtaken: Boats being overtaken have the right of way over the overtaking vessel, even when the slower boat is power and the faster boat is sail.

Restricted maneuverability: Boats with restricted maneuverability, whether due to fishing, draft, length, towing, or other causes, have the right of way over vessels not so restricted.

Traffic separation: Vessels participating in a traffic-separation scheme have the right of way over upriver and crossing vessels. (If you must cross a traffic lane, try doing so at right angles.)

Downriver: On certain inland waters, powerboats proceeding downriver have the right of way over upriver and crossing vessels.

Man-powered beats sail beats motorboat beats seaplane. Human-powered boats (such as canoes and rowboats) have the right of way over sailboats, which in turn have the right of way over powerboats, which have the right of way over seaplanes. The more technology your vessel has, the more you need to yield to those with less technology.

Starboard boat or starboard tack wins. If one boat is sail and one is power, the rule given above applies. For powerboats, the boat approaching from starboard has the right of way, regardless of from where it is approaching.

Leeward boat wins. When two sailboats meet on the same tack, the leeward boat has the right of way over the windward boat.

OPTICS

Colors of the Spectrum

- **ROY G. BIV**

red	blue
orange	indigo
yellow	violet
green	

Color Mixtures

- **B**etter **g**et **r**efreshed **w**hen **y**our **m**om **c**omes **b**ack.

blue, **g**reen, **r**ed = **w**hite
yellow, **m**agenta, **c**yan = **b**lack

Note: The primary colors of light are blue, green, and red. Known also as additive colors, they combine to create total color (that is, white light). The secondary colors of paint are yellow, magenta, and cyan. Used to make most other shades, the secondary colors of paint absorb or subtract one primary color of light, reflecting the light of only the other two. When all three secondary or subtractive colors combine, there is no color or light to see (which makes black).

PHYSICS

The Speed of Light in Meters Per Second

In this device the number of the letters in each word represents a digit.

- Wc guarantee certainty, clearly referring to this light mnemonic.

299,792,458

Atomic Orbitals

- Sober physicists don't find giraffes hiding in kitchens.

s	g
p	h
d	i
f	k

Electromagnetic Spectrum (in Order of Decreasing Frequency)

- Guests experience unusual vibrations in my room.

gamma rays	infrared radiation
x-rays	microwaves
ultraviolet radiation	radio waves
visible light	

Maxwell Relations in Thermodynamics: Clockwise Order

- **G**ood **p**hysicists **h**ave studied **u**nder **v**ery **f**ine **t**eachers.

G=Gibbs free energy	U=internal energy
P=pressure	V=volume
H=enthalpy	F=Helmholtz free energy
S=entropy	T=temperature

Maxwell Relations in Thermodynamics: Left to Right Order

- **V**alid **f**acts and **t**heoretical **u**nderstanding **g**enerate **s**olutions to **h**ard **p**roblems.

V=volume	G=Gibbs free energy
F=Helmholtz free energy	S=entropy
T=temperature	H=enthalpy
U=internal energy	P=pressure

PSYCHIATRY

- -

Anorexia Nervosa[76]

- **I FEAR LARD.**

Image of one's body is distorted in perception
fear of gaining weight is intense
expected weight gains are not made
amenorrhea (3 consecutive menstrual cycles are missed)
refusal to gain weight
laxative use (characteristic of the binge-eating–purging type)
anhedonia (inability to experience joy)
restricting type
denial of weight loss or emaciated body shape

Antisocial Personality Disorder[77]

- **CALLOUS MAN**

   conduct disorder before age 15; current age at least 18
   antisocial and arrestable acts
   lies frequently
   lacunae; lacks a superego (conscience)
   obligations not honored
   unstable (can't plan ahead)
   safety of self and others ignored
   money problems (often fails to support spouse and children)
   aggressive and assaultive
   not occurring only during schizophrenia or mania

Avoidant Personality Disorder[78]

- **RIDICULE**

   restrained within relationships
   inhibited in interpersonal situations
   disapproval expected at work
   inadequate view of self
   criticism is expected in social situations
   unwilling to get involved
   longs for attachment to others
   embarrassment is the feared emotion

Borderline Personality Traits[79]

- **I RAISED A PAIN.**

   identity disturbance
   relationships are unstable
   abandonment frantically avoided (whether real or imagined)
   impulsivity
   suicidal gestures (threats, self-mutilation, and so on)
   emptiness
   dissociative symptoms
   affective instability

paranoid ideation (thoughts), stress-related and transient
anger is poorly controlled
idealization followed by devaluation
negativistic (self-defeating thoughts and behavior)

Bulimia Nervosa[80]

- **A BINGE**

average of 2 binges per week over 3 months
behavior after consumption compensates for ingestion
ingestion of large amounts of food (binge eating)
not occurring only during anorexia nervosa
guilt feelings after binge eating
evaluation of self is unduly based on appearance

Note: The compensatory behavior often includes laxatives,
diuretics, self-induced vomiting, exercise, and the surreptitious
use of thyroid medicine.

Dementia of the Alzheimer Type[81]

- **DEAR GRAMPA**

decline in social or occupational function
executive functioning declines
apraxia
rule out as causes delirium, substance use, and general
    medical conditions
gradual onset and continual decline
relatives (runs in families)
aphasia
memory impairment
personality changes can occur (disinhibition, exaggerated
    traits)
agnosia

Dependent Personality Disorder[82]

- **DARN HURT**

  disagreement is difficult to express
  advice is excessively needed
  responsibility for major areas is delegated to others
  nurturance is excessively sought
  helpless when alone
  unrealistically preoccupied with being left to care for self
  relationships are desperately sought (when an established
     one ends)
  tasks are difficult to initiate

Dysthymic Disorder[83]

- **HE TAILS.**

  hopelessness
  esteem is decreased
  two-year duration (minimum)
  appetite changes (up or down)
  indecisiveness
  lethargy, low energy
  sleep changes (increased or decreased)

Generalized Anxiety Disorder (GAD)[84]

- **I'M A FICKLE CASE.**

  impaired functioning (as in social or occupational situa-
     tions)
  muscle tension
  axis I condition, if coexisting, is not the focus of the anxiety
  fatigued
  irritable
  control of worry is difficult
  keyed up (edgy)
  lasts for at least 6 months and occurs more often than not

events and activities are the focus of the worry (not just a
   single focus)
concentration is impaired
anxiety is excessive
sleep disturbance
excluded causes are substance disorders and general
   medical conditions

Note: Axis I conditions are major psychiatric syndromes or
clinical disorders.

Histrionic Personality Disorder[85]

- **I CRAVE SIN.**

inappropriate behavior (seductive or provocative)
center of attention
relationships are seen as closer than they really are
appearance is most important
vulnerable to others' suggestions
emotional expression is exaggerated
shifting emotions, shallow
impressionistic manner of speaking (lacks details)
novelty is craved

Narcissistic Personality Disorder[86]

- **A FAME GAME**

admiration required in excessive amounts
fantasizes about unlimited success, brilliance, attention
arrogant
manipulative
envious of others
grandiose sense of importance
associates with special people
me-first attitude
empathy lacking for others

Obsessive–Compulsive Disorder[87]

- **A BIT FORCED**

  attempts are made to ignore or suppress obsessions
  behavior isn't realistically connected with the obsession
  interferes with one's normal routine (social or occupational functioning)
  time-consuming (taking up at least 1 hour per day)
  feels anxious (anxiety)
  obsessions
  recognizes obsessions are self-induced
  compulsions
  excessive nature of obsessions and compulsions is appreciated
  distressing to the patient (ego-dystonic)

Obsessive–Compulsive Personality[88]

- **LOW MIRTH**

  leisure activity minimal
  organizational focus
  work and productivity predominate
  miserly spending habits
  inflexible about morals and values
  rigidity and stubbornness
  task completion impaired, especially because of perfectionism
  hoards items (can't discard them)

Panic Attack/Panic Disorder[89]

- **THIS ISN'T FUN.**

  trembling
  hot flashes
  increased heart rate
  sweating

inspiration (intake of air feels obstructed, creating a
    choking sensation)
smothering/shortness of breath
numbness or tingling in the limbs
tightness in the chest
fear of losing control, going crazy, or dying
unreal sense of self and the environment
nausea or abdominal distress

Phobic Disorders[90]

- **FEARED**

fear that is excessive and unreasonable
exposure to the stimulus provokes anxiety
avoids the phobic situation or object
recognizes that the fear is excessive
exclusion of other mental disorders, such as obsessive-
    compulsive disorder and post-traumatic stress syndrome
distress is experienced in the feared situation

Post-Traumatic Stress Disorder[91]

- **PRIDE AFRAID CHAINS**

physiological reactivity when exposed to cues
recollections of the events that are distressing
internal cues cause distress (symbolic reminders)
dreams of the event that are distressing
external cues cause distress
avoids stimuli associated with the trauma
foreshortened future (has no long-term goals)
recall of the event is impaired
affect has a restricted range
interest in activities is diminished
detached from others
concentration is impaired
hypervigilance
angry outbursts

impairment in social and occupational functioning
nocturnal problems (as in falling or staying asleep)
startle response (exaggerated reactions)

Most Common Psychoanalytic Techniques[92]

- **AFRAID**

analysis of resistance   interpretation
free association   dream analysis
analysis of transference

RELIGION

JUDAISM AND CHRISTIANITY

Hebrew Patriarchs

- **Abraham** (the founding patriarch) was the father of **Isaac**, who was the father of **Jacob**, who was the father of **Joseph**.

Chronological order=alphabetical order

7 Minor Hebrew Prophets (in Order of Appearance in the King James Bible)[93]

- **H**ow **j**ust **a**nd **o**bedient **J**onah **m**ade **N**ineveh.

Hosea   Jonah
Joel   Micah
Amos   Nahum
Obadiah

Old Testament/Hebrew Bible: The Torah (First 5 Books)

- George's evening lessons never dull.

Genesis

Numbers

Exodus

Deuteronomy

Leviticus

Passover: 10 Plagues[94]

- Before folks let Moses flee, beastly happenings loosed dreadful fears.

blood

boils

frogs

hail

lice

locusts

murrain (pestilence)

darkness

flies

firstborn killed

Hebrew Scriptures: Apocryphal Books

- T. J. McWeb, D.E.

Tobit

Ecclesiasticus

Judith

Baruch

Maccabees

Daniel (additions)

Wisdom of Solomon

Esther (additions)

The Ten Commandments

- Thou no God shalt have but me;
  Before no idol bow the knee;
  Take not the name of God in vain
  Nor dare the Sabbath day profane;
  Give both thy parents honor due;
  Take heed that thou no murder do;
  Abstain from words and deeds unclean
  Nor steal, though thou art poor and mean;
  Nor make a willful lie, nor love it,
  What is thy neighbor's, do not covet.

New Testament: Books

- Matthew, Mark, Luke, and John wrote the life of their Lord;
  The Acts, what Apostles accomplished, record;
  Rome, Corinth, Galatian, Ephesus hear
  What Philippians, Colossians, Thessalonians revere:
  Timothy, Titus, Philemon precede
  The Epistle which Hebrews most gratefully read;
  James, Peter, and John, with the short letter Jude,
  The rounds of Divine Revelation conclude.

New Testament: Order of Galatians, Ephesians, Philippians, and Colossians

- **G**eneral **E**lectric **P**ower **C**ompany

The Four Gospels

- Matthew, Mark, Luke, and John went to bed with their trousers on!

Book of Revelation: The Four Horseman of the Apocalypse

- **P**rophets **d**on't **w**elcome **f**ools.

Pestilence	War
Death	Famine

Roman Catholic Church: 4 Types of Prayer

- **ACTS**

adoration	thanksgiving
contrition	supplication

- **RAPT**

repentance	petition
adoration	thanksgiving

Sundays between Easter and Pentecost: Latin Names

- Quiet Master Dick Jones couldn't read any English.

Quasimodogeniti	Cantate
Misericordias	Rogate
Domini	Ascension
Jubilate	Exaudi

Note: Ascension falls on a Thursday.

The 12 Apostles

- This is the way the disciples run.
  Peter, Andrew, James, and
  John, Philip, and Bartholomew,
  Thomas next and Matthew too,
  James the less and Judas the
  Greater, Simon the zealot, and
  Judas the traitor.

Calvinism : 5 Tenets

- **TULIP**

total depravity	irresistible grace
unconditional election	perseverance of the saints
limited atonement	

7 Deadly Sins

- **PWELGAS**
- **WASPLEG**
- **LEWSGAP**

pride	gluttony
wrath	avarice
envy	sloth
lust	

7 Virtues

- For high court judge, pity tempers force.

faith	prudence
hope	temperance
charity	fortitude
justice	

4 Cardinal Virtues[95]

- Try putting justice first.

temperance	justice
prudence	fortitude

9 Orders of Angels

- Seraphim, Cherubim
  Come take your Throne
  Dominions and Virtues—
  Their Powers alone.
  Angels, Archangels,
  Next he sees,
  Seated along side
  Principalities.

Islam: Founder and 2 Holiest Cities

- 3 Ms

  Mohammed
  Medina
  Mecca

Note: Mohammed was the founder of Islam. Medina is where Mohammed settled in and died. Mecca is Mohammed's birthplace, where every Muslim is supposed to visit at least once.

CONFUCIANISM

Goals of Character and Social Life[96]

- **Gen**tle **C**onfucius **l**oved **t**he **w**orld.

GOAL	DEFINITION
jen	ideal relationship among people
chun-tzu	true manhood
li	propriety, ritual of a well-conducted life
te	power, arts of war
wen	culture, arts of peace

HINDUISM

4 Ways to God

- **J**hanas **b**ring **k**nowledge **r**eadily.

YOGA	GOAL
Jnana	the way to God through transcendental knowledge
Bhakti	the way to God through love or devotion
Karma	the way to God through work or selfless action
Raja	the way to God through psychological exercise

SIKHISM

Proper Appearance

- 5 Ks

  Kesh (hair must be uncut and in a turban)
  Kangha/Kanga (comb for keeping hair clean)
  Kaccha/Katchera/Kachera (white shorts worn under clothes)
  Kirpan (sabre)
  Kara (bracelet of steel worn on right wrist)

SPANISH

21 Common Spanish Verbs[97]

VERB (TRANSLATION)	PRONUNCIATION	MNEMONIC SENTENCE
aprender (to learn)	ah-prehn-DEHR	An **appren**tice **learns** from more experienced workers.
atender (to attend to)	ah-tehn-DEHR	An **attend**ant **attends to** people's nourishment.
beber (to drink)	beh-BEHR	Bob **drinks** coffee while others im**bib**e soft drinks.
cantar (to sing)	kahn-TAHR	Bing **can't sing**.

VERB (TRANSLATION)	PRONUNCIATION	MNEMONIC SENTENCE
comenzar (to begin)	koh-mehn-SAHR	We must **begin** **commen**cement exercises if we are to graduate.
comprender (to understand)	kohm-prehn-DEHR	Tests of reading **compre**hension measure whether people **understand** the material.
conducer (to drive)	kohn-doo-SEER	El **conduc**tor **drives** the instructors.
construir (to build)	kohn-stru-EER	The men **con-stru**cted the **building**.
contestar (to answer)	kohn-tehs-TAHR	The **contest**ant needed to **answer** the questions.
creer (to believe)	kreh-HER	Religions usually require people to **believe** various **cree**ds.
dormir (to sleep)	dohr-MEER	Norm **sleeps** in the **dorm**.
durar (to last)	doo-RAHR	**Dura**ble things **last** forever.
escribir (to write)	ehs-kree-BEER	Mike **scrib**bles when he **writes**.
fumar (to smoke)	fuh-MAHR	The **fum**es from their **smoking** made us cough.
mirar (to look at)	mee-RAHR	A **mir**age is some something people **look at**.
odiar (to hate)	oh-dee-AHR	I **hate** body **od**or.

VERB (TRANSLATION)	PRONUNCIATION	MNEMONIC SENTENCE
pensar (to think)	pehn-SAHR	**Pens**ive people **think** a lot.
recordar (to remember)	rreh-kohr-DAHR	Flo doesn't **remember** how to **record** her show.
saludar (to greet)	sah-loo-DAHR	The recruits **greet** me with a **salute**.
terminar (to end)	tehr-mee-NAHR	Roger's employment will **end** when his boss **termina**tes his position.
vender (to sell)	behn-DEHR	The **vend**ors **sell** their wares to customers.

SPELLING

A

absence: **Ken** certified the student's abs**en**ce.
abundance: **Lance** liked the abund**ance** of food.
academy: An academy is a place where you get an education.
accept (vs. except): A marine drill sergeant will **acc**ept anything **exc**ept e**xc**uses.
acceptable: **Accept** any **acceptable** ta**ble**.
accidentally: The car accident**ally** hit **Sally**.
accommodations: His garage can a**c**co**mm**odate two **c**ars and two **m**otorcycles.
accordion: The li**on** disliked accordi**on** music.
acquire: Ma**c** in**quire**d about the **quire** of paper.

acquit: **Zac quit** his job after he realized the jury would not **acquit** him.

ait (a small island): We bought b**ait** from a store on the **ait**.

albumen (egg white): The **men** consumed albu**men** for the prot**ein**.

aleph (first letter of the Hebrew alphabet): In the Hebrew al**ph**abet, ale**ph** comes first.

alien: A**lien**s may sometimes **lie** if they are here illegally.

alif (first letter of the Arabic alphabet): C**al**, **if** you learn Arabic, you'll need to recognize an **alif**.

align (to adjust to a proper position): You can't ali**gn** **gn**ats.

all right: To be **all** right, you need two *L*s and two words.

allude (to make an indirect reference): George began to **all**ude to **all** his children.

allusion (indirect reference): **All** his **all**usions were subtle references.

a lot (a large quantity): It takes **a lot** of money to own **a lot** filled with cars.

altar (a table for sacred purposes): The special t**able** was an alt**ar**.

alter (to change): Don't al**ter** the **ter**ms of my contract.

amateur: Robert is a **Eu**ropean amat**eur**.

amendment: The a**mend**ment can't **mend** human nature.

analyst: The anal**yst** examined the bo**y**.

analyze: The vet will anal**yze** the to**y** **ze**bra for accuracy.

androgynous (having both male and female characteristics): The andr**ogy**nous man smoked a st**ogy**.

annalist (writer of historical records): **Anna**, **list** the remarks of the **annalist**.

annuity: **Ann** enjoyed earning the **ann**uity.

annul (to make or declare void): Please don't **annul** the **annu**al election.

anoint (to apply oil to, as in a religious ceremony): To **ano**int is to use **an o**il.

apostle (one sent to preach the Gospel): Please **post** the words of the a**post**le.

apparel: Please replace the zi**pp**ers in the **el**even bags of a**pp**ar**el**.

apparent: The student was a**pp**ar**ent**ly ha**pp**y about not having to pay **rent**.

arc (a segment of a curve; an electrical current): The n**arc** asked the geometry student to describe an **arc**.

architect: The **arch** was designed by the **arch**itect.

argument: I lost an *E* in an arg**um**ent.

arithmetic: **A r**at **i**n **t**he **h**ouse **m**ay **e**at **t**he **i**ce **c**ream.

armoire (tall wardrobe or cupboard): In the room of the ch**oir E**d didn't expect to see an arm**oire**.

arraign (to call before a court of law): **Ign**atius, the ben**ign** ens**ign**, knew the grand jury would arra**ign** him.

arrant (extreme, especially in a negative sense): The speech was an **array** of **arra**nt nonsense.

array (to put in a desired order): **Arra**nge your schedule to **arra**y your soldiers for inspection.

asinine: It is **a sin** for a minister to be **asin**ine.

assassin: An **assass**in is a double **ass**.

assay (to test or evaluate): When you **ass**ay the movies, please don't call the director an **ass**.

assume: To a**ss**ume is to make an **ass** of **u** and **me**.

asterisk: Is there a **risk** of misplacing the aste**risk**?

athlete: After her b**ath let** the **athl**ete rest.

attendance: **At ten** people took **attendance** for the **dance**.

auger (tool for boring holes in wood or ice): A carpenter uses an aug**er**.

augur (to predict or foreshadow): Will he aug**ur four** events?

aural (pertaining to the ear or sound): To appreciate the cul**tural** achievement of the symphony required a**ural** sensitivity.

auteur (film director who dominates a movie's style): The aut**eur** was no amat**eur** director.

auxiliary (assisting): In private, the politician would refer to his running mate as a useful auxi**liary liar**.

aweful (inspiring adoration, worship, or dread): How can one be car**eful** when overcome by aw**eful** events?

awful (terrible): The **awful** action was far from l**awful**.

a while (an indefinite period of time): Sar**a w**ants to relax for **a** while.

awhile (for a short time): **Aw**fully tired, she rested **awh**ile.

awl (tool used to pierce small holes): When Ron was injured by the **awl**, he began to b**awl**.

axel (jump in figure skating): Eth**el** took a fall during an ax**el**.

axle (shaft around which wheels revolve): **Lex** broke the ax**le** on his front wheel.

B

baboon: The **bab**oon acted like a **bab**y.

bachelor: J. S. **Bach** did not remain a **bach**elor.

ba**il** (security, money): He needed the ba**il** to get out of ja**il**.

ba**le** (large bundle): It took a strong m**ale** to lift the b**ale** of hay.

ba**lk**y (uncooperative; contrary): **Al** was ba**lk**y whenever he didn't get his way.

ba**ll**oon: A **ball**oon is shaped like a **ball**.

ba**lm** (soothing lotion): I began to c**alm** down after the nurse applied the b**alm** to my back.

ba**na**na: **Ban a na**ked body, but not a **banana**.

b**are** (without covering): Michelle never did c**are** when her husband went b**are** around the house.

bar**gain**: Everyone can **gain** in the bar**gain**.

b**ar on** (nobleman): The **bar on** the door showed that the **baron** wanted privacy.

bar**que** (sailing ship): For Brad's sailing **que**st, he bought a bar**que**.

bar**re** (wooden railing used for ballet practice): After the ballerinas left, the **barre** was **barre**n.

bar**re**n (bare; empty): The police **arre**sted the criminal in a b**arre**n field.

basic**ally**: Basic**ally**, you need to meet me at a **rally**.

bas**il** (herb): When the spaghetti sauce started bo**il**ing, I added some bas**il**.

b**ass** (male singer of the lowest vocal range): The man who sang b**ass** was a pompous **ass**.

ba**tt**a**l**ion: The ba**tt**a**l**ion was tired of ba**ttle**.

batter**ie** (ballet movement): Barb**ie** hurt her feet while performing a batter**ie**.

b**awl** (to cry out loudly): When the children made fun of Bill's dr**awl**, he began to b**awl**.

ba**zaar** (market): If I graded the ba**zaar**, I'd give it three **A**s.

because: **B**ig **e**lephants **c**an **a**lways **u**se **s**mall **e**lephants.

b**eech** (tree): A b**eech** is a tr**ee**.

be**gg**ar: The be**gg**ar didn't go f**ar**.

b**eige** (light grayish or yellowish brown): My n**eig**hbor wore b**eige**.

believable: **Eva** wasn't beli**eva**ble.

benefited: The lecture benefi**ted Ted**.

ber**et** (small cap): The h**eret**ic wore a b**eret**.

bi**ann**ual (twice a year): **Ann** attended the bi**ann**ual event every February and September.

bi**enni**al (once every two years): **Denni**s was a representative subject to bi**enni**al elections.

b**ier** (stand on which a corpse or coffin is placed): We weren't sure which corpse would l**ie** on the b**ier**.

binoculars: The **bin** contained the **bin**oculars.

b**iz**arre (odd): The arrest of Mel Gibson in 2006 was a **bizarre** show-**biz arre**st.

bl**eat** (to cry plaintively): I left my s**eat** when I heard the wounded animal bl**eat**.

b**oar** (male pig): They beat the b**oar** with an **oar**.

bomb**e** (confection or frozen dessert): The cook made a num**be**r of bom**be**s.

boo**k k**eeper: The boo**k k**eeper's boo**k k**ept falling off the shelf.

b**ore**: We decided to b**ore** for **ore**.

b**ought**: We th**ought** you had b**ought** en**ough rough**age.

bo**uill**on (clear soup): Was **Lou ill** after the bo**uill**on?

- Bo**ui**llon is a like s**oui**p.

b**oul**der (very large rock): John hurt his sh**oul**der on the b**oul**der.

brass**ie** (golf club): Jake used his brass**ie** when he had a favorable l**ie** on the fairway.

br**ead**th (width): We **read** about the intellectual br**ead**th of Aristotle's interests.

br**eak** (to cause to come apart): If you br**eak** the pipe, it will spring a l**eak**.

br**illi**ant: The actor Jim Carrey is br**illi**ant in s**illi**ness.

bro**ccoli**: You should receive an a**ccol**ade for liking bro**ccoli**.

bro**chu**re (pamphlet): **Chu**ck brought the bro**chu**re.

br**ui**se: That a br**ui**se can r**ui**n a fr**ui**t is a tr**ui**sm.

br**ui**t (to spread news or rumors): Several people began to br**ui**t out rumors about the stolen fr**ui**t.

bru**net** (dark-haired male): **Set**h was the bru**net** at the **net**.

bru**nette** (dark-haired female): Jea**nette** was a bru**nette**.

bu**dget**: **Bud, get** your **budget** in order.

bu**oy** (floating object): The d**uo** watched the bu**oy**.

bureaucracy: **Ea**ch **u**ndertaker disliked the intri**cacy** of the bur**eaucracy**.

burglar: The **lar**ge burg**lar** was found guilty of **lar**ceny.

business: An honest bu**si**ness commits no **sin**.

C

cafeteria: It was s**afe** to eat in the **cafe**teria.

calendar: The calen**dar** was examined each **day**.

callous (without pity): Don't **call ou**t for help from **callou**s people.

callus (hardened patch of skin): **Call us** if you get a **callus**.

calorie: A calor**ie** doesn't l**ie**.

camouflage: They can find **out** the **age**nt's location because of his cam**ouflage**.

cancel: Let's not can**cel** the **cel**ery order.

candor (honest speech): **Or**son was known for his cand**or**.

cannon (mounted artillery): **Ann canno**t hear the **canno**n.

canoe: Don't leave your sh**oe** on the can**oe**.

canon (broad set of principles or set of authoritative writings): My professors preferred famous works in the philosophical c**anon** to **anon**ymous material.

canter (horse's gait between a trot and a gallop): An experienced rid**er** knows that a cant**er** is fast**er** than a trot.

cantor (church choir leader or singer of Jewish religious music): The cant**or** was also an instruct**or** at the temple.

canvas (coarse cloth): The artist Jackson Pollock liked to paint on a **vas**t can**vas**.

canvass (to survey): We need to canv**ass** the m**ass** of people.

capital (governmental city): We were bored by the empty **tal**k in the capi**tal**.

capital (money for a business): **Ca**sh is a form of capital.

capital (uppercase letter): John liked to use capi**tal**s to make **tal**l letters.

capitol (building where a legislature meets): Capit**ol** buildings often have d**o**mes.

■ The word *capitol* has **o**ne meaning.

capsule: The m**ule** walked over the caps**ule**.

caret (editing mark indicating the place for an insertion): The editor put **re**d marks and car**et**s on the manuscript.

caries (tooth decay): The rate of **caries** v**aries** from person to person.

car**ousel** (merry-go-round): The h**ouse** **L**arry bought was near a car**ousel**.

ca**rrel** (small cubicle used for individual study in a library): Bob saw a b**arrel** next to the c**arrel**.

cas**te** (hereditary, exclusive group based on rigid distinctions of birth or occupation): The cas**te** regarded associations with outsiders as a w**aste** of time.

cast**er** (wheel placed under furniture): A cast**er** is a wh**eel**.

cast**or** (oil used as a medicine or in perfume): Cast**or** is an **o**il.

cas**ua**lty (victim): Yo**u** **a**ren't **casual** about any **casual**ty of war.

cate**ch**ism (basic Christian beliefs or other instruction in a question-and-answer format): **C**harlene studied the cat-e**ch**ism in a **church** s**ch**ool.

category: My **cat** **eg**gs on the kittens.

- We **ate** food selected from a c**ate**gory on a Chinese menu.

ce**lestial** (heavenly): My astronomer pa**l** considered essen**tial** his knowledge of ce**lestial** bodies.

ce**llu**lose (component of plant cell walls): If you se**ll** the plant, you'll **lo**se the ce**llulo**se.

Celsi**us** (centigrade temperature scale): **C**arl **e**ats liver some-times **in** **u**gly **s**lippers.

cemetery: Ralph needed cement at a lot east of the cemetery.

- Stella cried "**Eee!**" as she passed the c**e**m**e**t**e**ry.

cens**er** (incense burner): The pot s**er**ved as a cens**er**.

cens**or** (person who deletes or suppresses ideas or materi-als): The cens**or** s**or**ted out material he considered offensive.

cens**ure** (blame; official rebuke): The corrupt senator was **sure** to receive cens**ure** from the Senate.

census (official count): **C**asey participated in the **cens**us.

ce**ss**ion (yielding or giving up rights or property): When the pupils misbehaved, there was a ce**ss**ion of rece**ss**.

ch**alice** (goblet or cup): **Alice** drank from the ch**alice**.

champ**agne** (sparkling white wine): **Agne**s loved the taste of champ**agne**.

chang**e**able (not staying the same): We are **able** to keep the **change** in **change**able.

chaplain (member of a clergy attached to a chapel): The heavy rain outside the chapel pained the chaplain.

charnel (place where dead bodies are kept): Elwood was the funeral worker in charge of the charnel.

chattel (movable property): Slaves, who had the legal status of chattel, sometimes sent telegrams.

chili (hot pepper): The Texan wanted chili in the Philippines.

chlamydia (disease): Henry was displeased to discover that he had contracted chlamydia.

choral (relating to a choir): The choral director loved working with the choir.

chorale (hymn or psalm that is sung): They'd listen to a chorale while drinking ale.

chord (music notes played together for harmony): Chuck learned to play chords.

Cincinnati: Cincinnati is a word, hard to spell but easily heard. It need not cause you irritation, just drop the *on* from *cin cin nation*.

cirrus (high, thin cloud): The cirrus cloud began to stir Rusty's imagination.

claque (group of hired applauders): The man who asked the question was a member of a claque.

clientele (customers): Please telephone the clientele.

cloche (woman's bell-shaped hat): The cloche was in the chest.

closure (anything that shuts or closes): After the two forgave each other, closure was sure.

cloture (vote of Congress to end a filibuster): Because we were unsure of the status of some votes, it was difficult to picture the cloture.

coarse (rough): The wood of the oar was coarse.

cocoa (chocolate drink): Vic spilled some cocoa on his coat.

coffer (treasury; strong box): We accepted her offer to add money to the coffer.

colonel (chief officer of a regiment): The lone colonel was sometimes lonely.

colossal: For Napoleon, Waterloo was a colossal loss.

coma (unconsciousness): They prayed for their friend to come out of the coma.

comedian (male comic): I saw the comedian standing on the median with his wife.

comma (kind of punctuation mark): **Comm**a errors are **comm**on even in college writing.

commitment: The co**mm**unis**t** wanted to **commit men t**o guard the northern border.

committed: The o**tt**er was co**mm**i**tt**ed to building a dam.

compatible: The religious man insisted that science is compat-**ible** with the **B**i**ble**.

complement: A comple**m**ent comple**t**es something.

compliment: A compl**i**ment is praise **I** enjoy.

comptroller (government official overseeing finances): The **compt**roller was a **promp**t administrator.

conscience (sense of right and wrong): **Science** needs a con**science**.

conscious: The **scio**n (descendant) was con**scio**us of his ancestry.

consensus (agreement): With no con**sensus** the judge may **send us** back into the jury room.

consul (government official): The citizen needed to **consul**t with the **consul**.

contributor: The contribut**or or**dered several pizzas.

control: Just **l**et them contro**l** the mob.

conveyance (action of transporting): We had enough mon**ey** for the conv**ey**ance of the goods.

coolly (in a cool or calm manner): M**olly** responded coo**lly** to the emergency.

coquette (flirt): The co**quette**'s flirting violated eti**quette**.

coral (underwater growth): **Cora** loved talking about the **cora**l reef.

corporation: The book concerned the **or**igin of the c**or**por**a**-tion.

corps (group of workers or soldiers): Some members of the **corps** saw the **corps**e.

corral (enclosure for animals): We needed to rea**rra**nge the co**rra**l to protect the animals.

cote (shelter for animals or birds, such as doves): We decided to v**ote** for building a **cote** for the birds.

council (legislative body): All members of each **ci**ty coun**cil** must be **ci**tizens.

counsel (to give advice): Wilma ignored Fred's wis**e** couns**e**l.

courageous: **Geo**rge was coura**geo**us when he drove his **Geo**.

courteous: The lawyers were **court**eous in **court**.

crevasse (major crack in large ice formations): We decided to can**vass** **e**veryone about the cre**vasse**.

criticism: The **critic** was known for his harsh **critic**ism.

cupboard (cabinet for storing food and utensils): He put a **cup** into the **cup**board.

curiosity: Curiosity will seldom **sit** idle.

currant (berry that when dried resembles a raisin): The curr**an**t looked like a **ra**isin.

curriculum (course of study): To graduate from college under four years will require you to h**urr**y through the c**urr**iculum.

cygnet (young swan): La**cy** liked the **cy**gnet.

D

debris (fragments; scattered remains): **Deb ris**es to remove the **debris**.

decision: **C**indy agreed with **Sid**'s de**cis**ion.

deficiency: The lack of respect for diverse cultural practices was an an**cien**t defi**cien**cy.

definite: We'll set a date when we can be defin**ite** about **it**.

dehydrate: If people don't get enough of the compound of **hy**drogen and oxygen known as water, they will be de**hy**drated.

demeanor (behavior, especially toward others): We noticed **Or**son's modest demean**or**.

demur (to take exception): The second doctor wanted to **demur** from the previous prognosis of the **femur**.

dependent: We were depend**ent** on Pam's **rent** paym**ent**.

depot (railroad or bus station; warehouse): The young man brought **pot** to the bus de**pot**.

desert (dry, barren wilderness): *Sahara*, *desert* and *sand* have only one *S* each.

desiccate (to dry out thoroughly): He **sicc**ed his dogs on a de**sicc**ated old man.

desirable: **Rab**ies is far from desi**rab**le.

despise: We need to **rise** above the urge to des**pise** others.

desserts (sweet food after a meal): The word *desserts* spelled backward is *stressed*.

- The two *S*s in *dessert* remind you to go for second*s*.

develop: Develop the film until you must st**op**.

devise (to invent): **D**enny devised a devious plan.

dinghy (small boat): **H**enry's dinghy was enjoyable when the tide was calm.

dingy (shabby; grimy; dull): Her ma**ngy** rug was in a di**ngy** apartment.

disbursement: **U**rge **S**erena to receive the earliest disbursement of funds.

discreet (showing tact): The teen was discreet about his controversial opinions.

discrepancy (failure to match): **Dis**cover the **dis**crepancy at once.

discrete (distinct, separate): **Crete** is a discrete place.

disguise: Our **gui**de **s**et out in a disguise.

disparate (quite different or distinct): Jill and **N**ate held disparate views.

doughty (brave): The boxer was rough and doughty.

drunkenness: Drunken neighbors can be rude because of their drunkenness.

duress (compulsion by threat): They could barely endure the duress.

dyeing (process of coloring with dye): When dyeing your clothes, be sure to leave the dye in.

dying (process of giving up life): Many people exaggerate the risk of dying while flying.

E

easel (tripod used by artists): The easel can be set up with ease.

ecstasy: The eclair Steve ate gave him ecstasy.

effect (to bring about): Much effort is needed to effect major change.

eighth: Eight heroes were interviewed on the eighth day of the war.

either: At the height of our leisure, we'd neither forfeit protein shakes nor seize either counterfeit money or weird drugs from foreign dignitaries.

eliminate: Inga decided to eliminate the waste.

elusion (act of escaping capture): Jeremiah's **elu**sion required him to stay at an obscure mot**el**.

embarrassing: Omitting the double *R* and double *S* can be doubly emb**arras**sing, especially for **r**eally **r**igorous, **s**erious **s**tudents.

embe**zz**lement (fraudulent appropriation of property): The office was abu**zz** with talk of the embe**zz**lement.

emigrate (to leave one's native country): The acad**emi**c wanted to **emi**grate from England to the United States.

emin**ent** (prominent, outstanding): The emin**ent** man was promin**ent** in the community.

em**oll**ient (substance for soothing or softening the skin): **Moll**y applied em**oll**ient to Bob's tired feet.

encore: The **en**core **en**abled the singer to show his talent again.

en**cy**clopedia: Lu**cy** loved reading the en**cy**clopedia.

end**orse**ment: The jockey gave us an end**orse**ment of the h**orse**.

enervate (to weaken): After Sylvia was **ener**vated, she had no **ener**gy.

enterp**rise**: Everyone was impressed by the **rise** of free enterp**rise** zones in the poor neighborhoods.

envel**ope** (a container for a letter): One doesn't need **rope** to seal an envel**ope**.

envi**ron**ment: **Ron** came from a stressful envi**ron**ment.

et cetera (and so forth): My p**et c**at doesn't know that the expression *et cetera* has two distinct parts.

eti**quette** (conduct defined as good manners): Tom's breaking into the **que**ue at church while smoking a cigar**ette** violated rules of eti**quette**.

exa**gger**ate: **G**oofy **G**ar**y** loved to exa**gger**ate.

ex**ceed**: If people are to pro**ceed** to college and suc**ceed**, they must ex**ceed** minimal academic standards.

ex**cell**ent: Ralph wanted to **exc**eed the speed limit without an **exc**ellent **exc**use.

except (other than): The teacher accepted no **exc**use **exc**ept illness.

ex**cess**ive: There is no **exc**use for **exc**essive drinking.

ex**cus**able: **Exc**eeding the speed limit just to buy a **sable** is not ex**cus**able.

exercise: **Wise** people know how to **exer**t themselves for **exer**cise.

existence: We knew nothing about the exi**sten**ce of **ten ten**ts.

exorcise (to drive out demons): The priest **or**ganized a plan to ex**or**cise the boy.

extemporaneous (without planning): The re**por**t was hid**eous** and extem**por**an**eous**.

extr**aor**dinary: His **aor**ta did an extr**aor**dinary job.

ext**reme**: Amputating a limb is sometimes a **reme**dy too ext**reme** to be used.

F

fak**ir** (Muslim ascetic): The fak**ir** didn't appreciate the woman's low-cut s**kir**t.

famil**iar**: The **liar** was famil**iar** with what people would believe.

f**are** (toll; fee): **Are** you happy with the f**are** you had to pay?

fa**scin**ation: Some people have a fa**scin**ation for clever **scam**s.

fea**sible**: **Ea**ch missionary considered the miracles of the **Bible** fea**sible**.

February: **Bring** your heavy coat for February.

fei**gn** (to pretend): **Eig**ht students decided to fei**gn** illness.

feint (to deceive or trick): Joan's n**eig**hbor feinted a rush.

fe**rrule** (band or cap enclosing the end of a cane; the protective point or knob on the far end of an umbrella): Our father would ov**errule** us by pointing the fe**rrule** of his umbrella at us.

fe**rry** (boat designed to transport people or goods across a stretch of water): **Terry** rode the fe**rry** across the river.

fe**rule** (a rod or ruler for punishing school children): The teacher enforced his **rule** with a fe**rule**.

fiery: He didn't want to l**ie** about the f**ie**ry explosion.

fi**let** (lace with a simple pattern; a special steak: filet mignon): We gave the fi**let** mignon to Fred to r**ile** Mandy.

fi**llet** (thin steak or strip of boneless meat or fish): After the ba**llet**, we had a fish fi**llet**.

fl**air** (aptitude): The man had a fl**air** for armch**air** speculation.

fla**re** (device for producing light): The fla**re** produced a fi**re**.

flexible: The man was seen as too flex**ible** in interpreting the **Bib**le.

floe (mass of glacial ice): M**oe** was impressed by the ice fl**oe**.

flu (influenza): Hearing a **flu**te doesn't call the **flu**.

fluorescent: Liq**uor** could be **sc**ary if it were fl**uor**escent.

forcible: Conversions to **Bib**lical faith should never be forc**ible**.

foreclosure: We paid the mortgage be**fore** the due date to avoid **fore**closure.

forehead: The **fore**head is right be**fore** the front of the scalp.

foreign: At the h**eight** of our l**eisure**, we'd n**either** forf**eit** prot**ein** shakes nor s**eize** **ei**ther counterf**eit** money or w**eird** drugs from for**eign** dignitaries.

foreword (preface): The **foreword** was written be**fore word** of the book contract.

forth (onward): Please fill out the **for**m before going **for**th.

forthright: We praise you **for** having enough l**ight** to be **forth**r**ight**.

forty: You were **for**tunate to find **for**ty dollars in front of the **for**t.

forwarded: We for**war**ded the **oar** to the sailor.

foul (not fair; illegal): Don't f**oul** **ou**t.

fowl (poultry; type of bird): An **owl** is a f**owl**.

Frances (a girl's name): Franc**es** was h**er** name.

Francis (a boy's name): Franc**is** was h**is** name.

fr**iend**: A fr**iend** bought me a p**ie**.

- Fr**iend** to the **end**.
- You wouldn't want to **fri** the **end** of your **friend**.

fundamental: The ability to say *amen* even to tragedy is fund**amen**tal to many conceptions of spirituality.

G

ga**rret** (attic): The fe**rret** was lost in the ga**rret**.

g**auc**he (tactless, awkward): At the **auc**tion **he** was g**auc**he.

gel (jellylike mixture or substance): An an**gel** shouldn't need hair **gel**.

genie (magical being who grants wishes): In the dream a do**g** accompa**nie**d the **genie**.

gen**ius**: **I us**e the gen**ius** of modern technology.

genuine: The l**ine** of termites was a genu**ine** problem.

gerbil (small rodent often kept as a pet): **Gil**'s **ger**bil loved to play on an exercise wheel.

gherkin (small cucumber for pickling): **Her**b enjoyed eating g**her**kins.

gigantic: The **gi**ddy **gi**ant was **gi**gantic.

gist (essence of something said or written): **Gi**ve us just the **gi**st of the story.

gonorrhea (disease): Either my s**on or Rhea** has contracted g**onorrhea**.

government: A **govern**ment **govern**s.

governor: Either the govern**or or** his lieutenant should have **or**ganized the event.

graffiti (wall drawings): The crudeness of the gra**ffit**i began to a**ffect** the pedestrians.

graham: **Hal** h**ated ham** on gra**ham** crackers.

grammar: Will **Sam mar** his paper with bad gr**ammar**?

grateful: Be gr**ateful** that no one **ate** diseased fish from the g**ulf**.

gratuitous (unearned; unwarranted): Eating fr**uit** and a submarine sandwich at the funeral was tremend**ously** grat**uitous**.

gravel (mixture of pebbles and cement): We found some rocks and **gravel** on the **grave** listed on the map.

grievous: It was a gr**ievous** error to have shielded the mischie**vous** child from punishment.

grisly (horrible): The **sly** criminal committed a gri**sly** crime.

grizzly (grayish; a brownish yellow bear of great strength and fierceness): The picnic grounds were abu**zz** about the gri**zz**ly bear nearby.

guarantee: The **guar**antee is your fr**ee guar**d against defective products.

guitar: Please give some fr**uit** to the g**uit**ar player.

H

hail (to call or summon): Please h**ail** a t**axi**.

hale (to force to go): **Dale** was h**ale**d into court for nonpayment of child support.

handful: I need a hand**ful** of light bu**lb**s.

handsome (attractive): San**dy** was hand**some**.

hangar (shelter for an airplane): A han**gar** is like a **gar**age for planes.

hanger (device for hanging clothes): Jeff aroused his wife's **anger** when he threw his shirt on the floor after taking it from the h**anger**.

hansom (horse-drawn carriage): The man demanding the **ransom** left in a h**ansom**.

happened: I was **happy** that your pu**pp**y **happ**ened to be there.

harass (to bother): M**ar**vin was at the m**ass** when he began to h**arass** the woman.

hardware: They didn't c**are** if we bought material at the hardw**are** store.

hare (large rabbit-like long-eared mammal): The h**are** liked some ponies, but was afraid of the m**are**.

haul (to drag or pull): S**aul** needed to h**aul** around his musical instruments.

having: **Vin**ce was ha**vin**g a good time.

Hawaii: There's water ski**ii**ng in Hawa**ii**.

hazard: Bill realized that the li**zard** was a ha**zard**.

hearth (floor of a fireplace; one's home): We built our h**earth** on barren **earth**.

heaven: Jason wanted to le**a**d people to h**ea**ven.

hectic: The pic**nic** was hec**tic**.

height: At the h**eight** of our l**ei**sure, we'd n**ei**ther forf**eit** prot**ein** shakes nor s**eize** **ei**ther counterf**eit** money or w**eird** drugs from for**eig**n dignitaries.

heir (one next in line to inherit wealth): The h**eir**s renounced th**eir** wealth.

hem**orrhage** (excessive bleeding): **H**ank **e**ntered **m**y **o**ut-classed **r**ed **r**acehorse **h**elplessly **a**gainst **g**rand **e**quines.

her**oes**: People must keep on their t**oes** to become her**oes**.

heroine (heroic female; female protagonist of a story or novel): The hero**ine** was a woman unafraid of sw**ine**.

hideous: You must not **hide** from the **hide**ous truth.

hin**drance**: **Dra**b people rarely p**rance** around an ent**rance**, creating a hin**drance**.

hoard (to hide supplies): No sailor can s**oar** if he h**oar**ds all the **oar**s.

hoarse (low and rough in sound): The cheerleaders **roar**ed themselves h**oar**se.

holey (containing holes): When the monk**ey** got hold of the **hole** puncher, my papers were **holey**.

hom**oge**neous (of a similar kind or nature): Much of the humor of the Three Sto**oge**s and Jim Carrey is hom**oge**neous.

horde (wandering tribe or large, moving crowd): The police decided to **order** the h**orde** to disburse.

hos**iery** (stockings): Ste**lla** wore hos**iery** on the **pier**.

hos**tel** (inexpensive lodge, especially for traveling youth groups): Mon**tel** saved money by staying at a hos**tel** instead of a ho**tel**.

hos**tile**: If you **rile** my dog, he'll become hos**tile**.

hum**erus** (bone of the upper arm): The soldier injured his hum**erus** in **Jerus**alem.

Hung**ary** (European country): She bought her **gar**ment in Hung**ary**.

hur**tle** (to move quickly; to drive or move recklessly): Don't expect a tur**tle** to hur**tle**.

hyg**ie**ne: My analog**ie**s about hyg**ie**ne were funny.

hyperb**ole** (exaggeration): The boy's wh**ole** story contained hyperb**ole**.

hyp**ocrisy**: When people publicly endorse high standards, they **risk** hyp**ocrisy**.

I

id**le** (not working): We rarely saw the mu**le** id**le**.

id**ol** (object of devotion): Pagans built id**ol**s of their g**od**s.

id**yll** (poem about carefree, romantic episodes; delightful, peaceful experience, especially in the countryside): The **idyll** described a t**idy** **ll**ama living outside a country home.

ignor**ant**: The ignor**ant** man intentionally threw an **ant** into the woman's coffee.

ileum (part of the small intestine): Ben's digestive problems began when he had trouble with his **ile**um near the **Nile** River.

ilium (large pelvic bone): The damage to the **ili**um affected Sheldon's ab**ili**ty to walk.

illegi**ble** (incapable of being read): When Benny became **ill** from **gin**, his handwriting was **illegible**.

illicit (impermissible; illegal): The **ill**egal plan was so obviously **ill**icit that it made a participant **ill**.

illiterate (incapable of reading and writing): Molly would soon become **ill** on hearing that cannibals **ate ill**iterate tourists.

illuminate: B**ill** loved to **ill**uminate the Christmas tree.

illusion (deception; hallucination): Cheryl wanted to rid J**ill** of **ill**usions.

imitate: I sub**mit** that we should l**imit** our desire to **imit**ate to only good role models.

immediately: M**om ate imm**edi**ate**ly.

immigrant (person who moves into a country): T**imm**y liked the new **imm**igrant.

immigrate (to come to a new country to dwell or settle): To **imm**igrate into a country is to c**om**e and **m**ove there.

imminent (soon to happen): We **imm**ediately s**ent** word of an **imm**inent attack.

impat**iens** (annual flowering plant): The al**iens** we hired helped us plant impat**iens**.

impo**ssible**: The oppressive government tried to make it impo**ssible** to confe**ss** publicly belief in the B**ible**.

incident**ally** (by the way): Incident**ally**, **Wally** was at the r**ally**.

in**ci**pient (emerging, developing): Her in**cip**ient laziness foreshadowed her lack of future parti**cip**ation.

indepen**dent**: The political indepen**dent** made barely a **dent** in the election results.

in**dict** (to charge with a crime): The grand jury was about to in**dict** the ad**dict**.

indiscr**ete** (not separated or divided into parts): The athl**ete** turned in an indiscr**ete** pile of papers.

indi**s**pens**able**: Heather **is** so **able** that she has become indi**s**pens**able**.

ind**ite** (to make up or compose, as a poem or story): To ind**ite** a message to a friend is to wr**ite** it.

inevi**table** (unavoidable): Buying a new **table** was inevi**table**.

in**fi**nite (without limits): We wanted to **fi**ni**s**h **te**aching about the in**fi**nite.

infla**mm**able (easily set on fire): It is a bu**mm**er to misuse infla**mm**able chemicals.

ingen**ious** (clever): Cind**i ou**tplayed even her ingen**ious** opponent.

innate (inborn): Was the man's **inn**er drive **inn**ate?

innovate (to introduce something new): **Minn**ie loved to **inn**ovate at the **inn**.

inoculate (to inject): To **in**oculate the child against certain diseases, we needed to give her an **in**jection.

insistent: Jason was **insis**tent about the **tent**.

insolate (to expose to the sun): **Sol** decided to **insol**ate the fruit to help it ripen.

instead: The gym instructor asked us to drink water **inst**ead of **tea**.

instructor: The **instruct**or **or**dered the students to sit down.

insulate (to separate or shield, especially to prevent the transfer of electricity, heat, or sound): We went under the tree to **insu**late us from the **su**n.

intercede (to intervene): We ra**ce**d **e**ach day to see who would **interce**de first on the child's behalf.

interfere: **Here** Bob might interf**ere**.

interpret: Let's **pret**end we shall not need to inter**pret** the message.

interru**pt**: It is an **err**or to inter**rupt** a person in the middle of a sentence.

interstate (between states): We forgot to **enter** the **interstate** highway.

intrastate (within a state): **Ray** conducted only **intra**state commerce.

inure (to get used to something, especially something unpleasant): The **Inu**its are **inu**red to cold weather.

irreparable (incapable of being repaired): Osca**r** **r**esisted **para**noid theories about **irrepara**ble harm to our nation.

irresistible: Lipstick made Barbara irres**istible**.

islet (small island): An **isl**et **is** a small **isl**and.

isosceles (having two equal sides): Was **Osc**ar's **ele**phant **isosceles**?

it's (contraction of "it is"): *Aid for use:* Can you meaningfully substitute "it is"? It's [It is] raining.

itinerary (plan; course of travel): Almost any sold**ier** would find sc**ary** the new itin**erary**.

its (possessive of it): The cat f**its** **its** bed. [See *it's*.]

J

jamb (post forming the side of a door or window): The **j**am**b** of the door was painted **amb**er.

jeopardi**ze** (to endanger): When **L**e**o z**agged the car, he **jeo**pardized his safety.

jinx (bad luck; a source of bad luck): We didn't consider an image of the Sph**inx** either a charm or a **jinx**.

jo**ule** (measure of energy): The student **foule**d up his calculations of **joule**s.

judicious (wise): At **C**indy's h**ouse**, we needed to be judi**cious**.

jun**ta** (council for governmental purposes; small group ruling a country, especially after a coup): The **jun**ta removed **jun**kies from the government.

justifiable: **Mia** had no justif**iable** excuse.

K

karting (sport of racing with karts, that is, lightweight vehicles): **K**arl loved the sport of **k**arting.

ker**osene**: **C**li**o** refused her **ene**mies ker**osene**.

ket**ch** (small sailboat): **Ch**et loved sailing on his **k**et**ch**.

kiln (oven for hardening pottery): **Ja**n baked the clay pottery in the kil**n**.

kinderg**art**en: I met **B**art in kinderg**art**en, where we both learned **art**.

knave (deceitful, dishonest person): Because **K**en was a **kn**ave (not a **kn**ight), no one trusted him.

knea**d** (to work material with one's hands): **K**ay would first **read** the newspaper and then **kn**ead some dough.

knell (tolling of a bell; any mournful sound): We were carrying our **kn**apsacks as we heard the **kn**ell.

knowledge: You'll have an **edge** armed with the latest knowl**edge**.

L

ladd**ie** (lad or young boy): The ladd**ie** loved the p**ie**.

lade (to load, as onto a ship): The men would **l**ade the boats until they made the gr**ade** for a supervisory position.

lager (light beer): The young man accidentally spilled the **lag**er on the f**lag**.

laid (past tense of *lay*): My m**aid** was p**aid** once I l**aid** down $50.

lair (animal's home): It wasn't f**air** to disturb the animal's l**air**.

language: Della had an adeq**ua**te grasp of the lang**ua**ge.

larvae (plural of *larva*): The **ae**rial picture didn't yield a well-defined view of the larv**ae**.

latitude: As to the storm, we be**at it** because of our l**atit**ude.

latter (second of two things): The la**tte**r pu**tte**r is be**tte**r.

lawyer: Tom **Sawyer** was no l**awyer**.

league (association): When Crystal began to ar**gue** with the **gue**sts, she was out of her lea**gue**.

led (past tense of *lead*): Doris l**ed** her husband N**ed** to the r**ed** b**ed**.

lei (Hawaiian decorative necklace): The l**ei** around my neck doesn't w**ei**gh much.

leisure: At the h**ei**ght of our l**ei**sure, we'd n**ei**ther forf**ei**t prot**ei**n shakes nor s**ei**ze **ei**ther counterf**ei**t money or w**ei**rd drugs from for**ei**gn dignitaries.

liable (likely): **Liar**s are l**ia**ble to be unre**lia**ble.

liaison (connection): Mar**ia is** our l**iais**on.

library: Janice wore her new **bra** to the li**bra**ry.

- The li**bra**rian is a **Libra**.

license (official permission): The **cens**us **e**ach worker conducted required a li**cense**.

licorice (sweet black candy with flavoring from the licorice plant): Pouring lico**rice** flavoring into the **rice** was a mistake.

lien (legal claim): **I en**courage you to put a l**ien** against your debtor's house.

lieu (in place of): The l**ieu**tenant was there in l**ieu** of the captain.

lieutenant: The l**ieu**tenant chose to l**ie** to **u**s.

lightning (electrical flash in the sky): Egads! There's no *E* in ligh**tn**ing.

likelihood: **Li**sa will, in all like**li**hood, **li**ve in a **li**ttle house.

limousine (large, luxurious car): In front of Tom's h**ous**ing **E**d parked the lim**ousine**.

liquefy (to reduce to liquid): The **ref y**ou selected wanted to liqu**efy** the ice on the field. [See also "English Grammar and Pronunciation."]

liqueur (sweet alcoholic drink usually taken after a meal): The liqu**eur** we tasted during dessert was from **Eur**ope.

liquor (alcoholic beverage): After we had reached our **quo-rum**, someone wanted li**quor**.

littoral (pertaining to the seashore): The **attor**ney enjoyed his litt**oral** bungalow.

llama (a South American ruminant mammal): **L**isa loves her **ll**ama, which she keeps in the barn.

loneliness: When a**lone**, some people may be pr**one** to feelings of **lone**liness.

loose (not tight): Tie your m**oose** a bit l**oose**.

lose (to misplace): I'd l**ose** my n**ose** if it weren't attached to my face.

losing (misplacing): I'm enc**losing** advice about **losing** things.

loupe (small magnifying glass used by jewelers and watch-makers): The jeweler dropped his **loupe** into the canta**loupe** and later in someone's c**oupe**.

luggage: Do**ug g**ave me **g**ood l**ugg**age.

luxury: Re**x** wanted to b**ury** his bone in lu**xury**.

M

magazine: Ro**z ine**ptly edited the maga**zine**.

magnetic: Some portion of the plas**tic** contained a magne**tic** metal.

magnificent: The **cent**erpiece on the table was magnifi**cent**.

maintain: I visited Sp**ain** even during the r**ain** to m**ain**tain my ability to speak the language.

maintenance (upkeep): I **inten**d for ma**inten**ance to arrive at **ten**.

malaise (vague mental or physical discomfort): It is difficult to measure or appr**aise** something as intangible as mal**aise**.

malignant (evil in nature or influence): There was something malign**ant** about Trish's r**ant**.

manageable: If you are **able** to **manage** anything, you know it's **manage**able.

management: At what **age** were you promoted to man**age**ment?

mandrill (large baboon): We decided not to use an electric **drill** near the man**drill**.

maneuver (to manage, manipulate, or guide): The **man eu**logizing **Ver**a began to **maneuver** us to the grave site.

mannequin (model of a human body used by window dressers and tailors): Did you see the ma**nnequin** on **Mann**y's **equin**e?

mantel (shelf above a fireplace): The toy **el**ephant was on the mant**el**.

manufacture (to produce): We learned to **manu**facture the product with only a little **manu**al labor.

marquee (roof-like projection, often featuring a theater's name): We lined up in a **queue** near the mar**quee**.

marriage: **I** believe in marr**i**age.

marshal (law officer; to arrange in order): A mars**hal** was **hal**ing a criminal into court.

marshmallow: Sometimes a **mall** will sell marsh**mall**ows.

martial (relating to war or the military): The mart**ial** music was not heard at the **trial** because of its poten**tial** to arouse emotions.

Massachusetts: The simple answer to this little riddle: Two *S*s, two *T*s, with one *S* in the middle.

mathematics: The children wanted me to teach **them** math**em**atics after we sang the national an**them**.

maybe: **Maybe** your wish **may be** granted.

meanness (baseness; stinginess): **N**at's **n**itpicking revealed his mean**n**ess.

meant (past tense of *mean*): **Ea**ch word me**a**nt something different.

medallion: After the wizard pinned a **medal** on the roy**al lion**, I received my **medallion**.

medicine: The movie *The Hospital*, starring George C. Scott, examined medi**cine** through **cine**matic satire.

medieval (concerning the Middle Ages): **Me**n often wanted to **die val**iantly in med**ieval** tales.

mediocre (ordinary): Some members of the **cre**w were medio**cre**.

menace (to threaten): The woman carried m**ace** to men**ace** muggers.

merchandise (goods for sale): I'd ad**vise** against buying illegally obtained merchand**ise**.

merely (simply): Should Ro**me rely merely** on wavering opinion?

metallurgy (science of metals and metalwork): Dealing with only things **metall**ic, **metall**urgy doesn't concern b**all**oons.

mete (to dispense or hand out): The judge wanted to hear the comp**lete** evidence before he would m**ete** out justice.

meteor: He had an interesting th**eor**y about met**eor**s.

meticulous (timidly precise): The scholar studied all mira**culous** stories with meti**culous** attention.

mettle (courage, spirit, spiritedness): The alcoholic had enough me**ttle** to give up the bo**ttle**.

mien (air or bearing of a person): The illegal al**ien** had a distinguished m**ien**.

mileage: You always find at least one **mile** in the word *mileage*.

millennium (1,000 years): In 2001, **Denni**s celebrated the new mill**enni**um.

millinery (woman's hats; a business selling woman's hats): Milli**nery** stores s**erve** people's heads.

millionaire: The million**aire** owned an **Aire**dale terrier.

milquetoast (timid, meek, apologetic person): The mil**que**toast was always **que**stioning his own abilities and worth.

miner (worker in a mine): If you work in a m**ine**, you're a m**ine**r.

miniature: The cowboy used a lar**iat** to catch the min**iat**ure schnauzer.

minimum: After the earthquake, the people in the town did only a **mini**mum of **mini**ng in **mini**skirts.

minor (person under legal age; trivial): The min**or or** his parent must be in court.

minuscule (tiny amount or number): The quantity was so **minus**cule as almost to be a **minus** quantity.

minutes: We had only a few min**utes** to listen to the fl**utes**.

miscellaneous (mixed together): Scott'**s cell** phone was found among mi**scell**aneous objects.

mischievous (prankish): The child was too ner**vous** to be mischie**vous**.

missile (something thrown or shot): The m**issile** seemed to h**iss** for a m**ile**.

Mississippi: *M*, *I*, crooked letter, crooked letter, *I*, crooked letter, crooked letter, *I*, humpback, humpback, *I*.

- *M, I*, double *S, I*, double *S, I*, double humpback, *I*.
- Remember **Miss is sipp**ing.

Missouri: We all **miss our Missouri**.

misspell: Just copy **Miss Pell**, and you'll always correctly spell *misspell*.

moccasins (type of shoe): There are a great **m**any **occasi**ons for **moccasins**.

- **Can Carl** see my mo**cc**asins?

model: We saw the mod**el** in the hot**el**.

moisten (to make wet): Mois**ten** the meat until **ten**der.

monotonous (boring): We had to sc**oot on out** because the party was m**onotonou**s.

morale (spirit): **Dale** knew the s**ale** would boost his mor**ale**.

mortgage (pledge of property as security): **Mort** could easily afford his **mort**gage.

mosquito: **Mos**t people **quit** wearing shorts during **mosquit**o infestations.

mot (witty or pithy saying): My **mot**her gave us a different **mot** every day.

mourning (expressing grief): We had s**our** expressions as we were m**ourn**ing **our** father's death.

municipal (concerning a city): **Al** was our **pal** in munici**pal** government.

murmur (to make low, indistinct sounds): When the **mur**alist hurt his fe**mur**, he began to **murmur** an obscenity.

muscle: **Sc**ott packed on a lot of mu**sc**le and became mu**sc**ular.

museum: Please **use** a new f**use** at the m**use**um.

mustache: No one said your **mustache must ache**.

mysterious: I was anx**ious** about the myster**ious** phone call.

N

naive (unsophisticated; innocent): **Nay, I've** been n**ai**ve.

narrative (story): Carte**r** **r**ead the na**rr**ative.

naturally: Natu**rally**, **Sally** was an **ally** at the **rally**.

necessary: Is it ne**cess**ary to have **recess** in a **cess**pool?

necessity: Was it a ne**cess**ity to have a **cess**pool in the **city**?

neighbor: We couldn't believe the **height** and **weight** of our for**eign** n**eigh**bor.

neither: At the height of our leisure, we'd neither forfeit protein shakes nor seize either counterfeit money or weird drugs from foreign dignitaries.

neutron (uncharged elementary particle): The amateur had to bone up for his quiz on neutrons.

niece: My niece gave a piece of pie to a man who had achieved the rank of chief.

nineteen: You should have more than one phone line for nine teens.

ninety: Nine types of people attended ninety classes.

ninth: The ninth-place winner was announced before the tenth-place winner.

nobby (chic, stylish, excellent): The snobby boy loved his nobby clothes.

noes (plural of *no*): Does the president of our club count the noes of the voters.

noticeable: Good spellers are able to notice the *E* in noticeable.

nuisance (a source of irritation): The nuisance dropped fruit on my suit.

O

obedience: A strict diet requires obedience.

obliged: She felt obliged when someone offered her a light.

oboe: Don't throw a hoe at the oboe.

observant (watchful): A good servant is observant.

obstacle: Please clear the obstacle with your vehicle.

occasion: Come celebrate a special occasion.

occur: Accidents can occur in soccer.

occurrence: Cathy can arrest him for the occurrence.

official: I am lawful as a special official.

often: To lose nine out of ten times is too often.

omission: I understand your omission to discuss nuclear fission.

omitted: Matthew omitted taking my mitt.

only: We cannot remain actionless onlookers only.

opinion: What's your opinion of Pip's onion?

opponent: I was happy for each opponent.

opportunity: We need to be shopping for opportunity.

opposite: Often prosperous people open stores in the east.

oppression: We weren't ha**pp**y to hear about your s**ession** of o**ppression**.

optimism: Sl**im** and **Tim** were known for op**tim**ism.

orangutan: **Put an** orang**utan** on the blanket.

orchestra: I was on the **porch** near the **orch**estra.

ordinarily: Ordin**arily**, the dance is **airily** graceful.

oriel (upper-story bay window): Gab**riel** loved to look out the o**riel**.

origin: I'd like to know about the ori**gin** of **gin** rummy.

oriole (species of bird): The ori**ole** hid in the h**ole** of a tree.

outrageous: The electrical **outage** had **outrage**ous consequences.

overrate: Let's not ove**rr**ate the black che**rr**y soda.

overrule: La**rr**y decided to ove**rr**ule the other judges.

overrun: It was an e**rr**or to try to ove**rr**un our enemies.

P

pageant: **E**ach pag**ea**nt is different.

paid: He p**aid** the m**aid** for her **aid**.

palate (roof of the mouth): Joyce's **pal ate** some peanut butter, which got stuck to his **palate**.

pale (colorless): Each m**ale** drank **pale ale**.

palette (thin board used by an artist to mix paint): The pal**ette** is for paint, not cigar**ette**s.

pallet (bed; wooden platform used for loading heavy materials): My **pal let** me put some paint cans on a **pallet**.

pane (sheet of glass): His c**ane** shattered the p**ane**.

panicky: The blood from the shaving **nick** made John pan**ick**y.

parallel: Not **all** lines are par**all**el.

paralysis: **Y** (why) does your **sis**ter have paral**ysis**?

paralyze: **Y** (why) would you want **Z**eke to paral**yze** Carl? (See ANALYZE.)

pare (to remove the outer covering, as of an apple): She asked whether I'd **care** for her to p**are** an apple.

parley (conference, especially to resolve a dispute): The disputants began to surv**ey** opinion at the parl**ey**.

parliament: **I am ent**ering the parl**iament**.

partial: A **part**ial story is only a **part** of the whole.

particular: **Art**'s **car** was a par**ticular** shade of green.

passed (past tense of *pass*): His br**ass** cup was p**ass**ed around.

past (by): At **last**, I walked p**ast** the new building.

pastime: I have enjoyed different p**astime**s **as time** goes by.

patience: He had no pa**tie**nce to **tie** a complete knot.

patients (clients of dentists or medical doctors): Dentis**ts** help their patien**ts**.

pavilion (exhibition area): We saw a dande**lion**, but no **lion**, near the pavi**lion**.

peace (absence of discord; quiet): The Pacific Oc**ea**n got its name because it was considered a s**ea** of p**ea**ce.

peaceable (friendly): **Peace**able people are **able** to keep the **peace**.

peculiar (strange): Unfortunately, a **liar** in politics is not pecu**liar**.

pekoe (tea made from the youngest leaves): We wondered whether Michelle had ever put al**oe** juice in her pek**oe** tea.

penetrate: The fish couldn't pe**net**rate the **net**.

penicillin: When B**ill** became **ill**, he wanted penic**ill**in.

peninsula: I decided to o**pen in** a **penin**sula neighborhood.

perceive: I perc**ei**ve **ei**ght flowers.

performance: His per**formanc**e was **for man**kind.

permanent: A lion's **mane** is per**mane**nt.

permissible (allowed): **Is si**lk perm**i**ss**i**ble?

perseverance: It was an **era** of persev**era**nce.

persevere: **Here** and t**here** you must persev**ere**.

persistent: She was persis**tent** about paying r**ent** for the **tent**.

personal (private): **Sal** got person**al**.

personally: Person**ally**, I like the r**ally**.

personnel (people working on a job): My perso**nne**l are always su**nny**.

perspiration (sweat): **I ration** work, not persp**iration**.

persuade: We tried to pers**ua**de the intellect**ual** to change her mind.

petal (flower part): He dropped a **pet**al on the car**pet** of the florist's shop.

physician (doctor): **Ph**one **y**our **phy**sician about **physic**al therapy.

physique (build of one's body): **Y** (why) **que**st for the perfect phys**ique**?

piccolo (a flutelike musical instrument): We need to a**cc**ept the pi**cc**olo.

picnicking: We've never seen a **king** picnic**k**ing.

piece (part of something): Her n**ie**ce began to l**ie** about the p**ie**ce of p**ie**.

pigeon (kind of bird): Will a **pig** eat a p**eony** in front of a **pigeon**?

pilgrimage (trip): What made the pu**pil grim** during the **pilgrim**age?

pillar (column): Please put the **pill ar**tfully by the **pillar**.

pistil (female flower part): Our botany instructor called the pist**il** the "g**irly** part" of the flower.

pistol (small gun): He was sh**ot** by a pist**ol**.

pitiful: Cher**yl** had a pitiful excuse.

Pittsburgh (city in Pennsylvania): It was **h**eavenly to see the Pittsburg**h** Steelers win the Super Bowl.

plague (contagious epidemic disease): The **gue**st was exposed to the pla**gue**.

plaid (pattern of stripes crossing at right angles): He p**aid** for the p**laid** tie **laid** on the counter.

plane (airplane): If you want to catch a p**lane**, you'll need to get into the **lane** for the airport.

planned (arranged): The ba**nn**ing of the book had been pla**nn**ed.

plantar (pertaining to the sole of the foot): The young man had plant**ar war**ts on his feet.

playwright (dramatist): The play**wright wr**ote e**ight** plays.

pleasant: The **peas** had a p**leas**ant taste.

politician: They wanted to leave **politic**s to **politic**ians.

pomegranate (fruit): **Meg ate** the po**meg**ran**ate**.

populace (the common people; the masses): The popu**lace** won't like a politician who always wears **lace**.

porcelain (kind of ceramic): He had accidentally **lain** on the porce**lain** cup.

porpoise (dolphin): The por**poise** had beautiful **poise**.

posse (volunteer group formed to help law officers): The **posse posse**ssed legal authority to aid the sheriff.

possess (own): The tax collector will a**ssess** whatever you po**ssess**.

possibility: There's a po**ssib**ility that you might be a**ssig**ned a ger**bil**.

possible: It is po**ssib**le that I will a**ssign** your seat.

potat**oes**: You don't need to keep on your **toes** to distinguish toma**toes** from torped**oes**.

practic**ally** (almost): Our **ally** had practic**ally** no power.

prac**tice**: Betty had some prac**tice** hiding her facial **tic**.

pra**ir**ie (open grassland): We found some animal's l**air** in the open **air** of the pra**ir**ie.

pre**ced**e (to go before): **Ced**ric wanted to pre**ced**e me.

prec**ious** (of great value): **I** owe **us** a prec**ious** vacation.

pre**coc**ious (advanced): **Coco** was a pre**coc**ious girl.

pre**fer** (favor): I pre**fer Fer**gie's dress.

pref**ere**nce: It was m**ere** pref**ere**nce.

pre**ju**dice (bias): Those who **prejud**ge harbor **prejud**ice.

pre**par**ation: The **par**ty required pre**par**ation.

prev**al**ent (widespread): **Sal**es were prev**al**ent.

pre**y** (to hunt for food): Before **pre**dators **pre**pare to eat, they must **pre**y on other animals.

pri**mer** (introductory textbook): I began my studying with a **mere** pri**mer**.

primitive: Their methods weren't **prim** but **prim**itive.

princi**pal** (head of a school): The school princi**pal** is your **pal**.

principl**e** (rule): Honesty is the best ru**le** or principl**e**.

pri**vile**ge: It's **vile** that undeserving people have pri**vile**ges.

proce**d**ure: **Ted** understood the proce**d**ure.

pro**cee**d (to continue): Pro**cee**d at a slower sp**eed**, or you'll ex**ceed** the speed limit and won't suc**ceed**.

pro**dig**y (person of extraordinary talent or ability): The math pro**dig**y liked to **dig** into proofs.

profe**ss**ion: The vet's **profession** led him to **profess** love for the l**ion**.

pro**fess**or: The pro**fess**or will con**fess or** be questioned.

prom**ine**nt (important; famous): The w**ine** expert was prom**ine**nt.

pro**nou**nce: You need your m**ou**th to pro**nou**nce any **noun**.

pro**nun**ciation: We had f**un** listening to the **nun**'s pro**nun**ciation.

prophe**cy** (prediction): We couldn't believe the ra**cy** prophe**cy**.

prophe**s**y (to predict): The **s**eer liked to prophe**s**y.

prosecut**or**: That criminal needs both a prosecut**or** and an instruct**or**.

prot**ein**: At the h**eight** of our l**eis**ure, we'd n**eith**er forf**eit** prot**ein** shakes nor s**eiz**e **eith**er counterf**eit** money or w**eir**d drugs from for**eig**n dignitaries.

psychology: **Pass y**our **psy**chology book.

publi**cly**: **Cly**de publi**cly** selected his assistant.
  [Note: *Publicly* is the only English adverb from a word
  ending in -*ic* that doesn't form the adverbial form by adding
  -*ally*, such as *artistically*, *statistically*, and *romantically*.]

pun**dit** (learned person, especially one who gives public
  commentary): The pun**dit** spoke about cre**dit** rates.

purchase: The sales talk tended to s**pur** my **pur**chase.

pursue (to go after): The **pur**ist liked to **pur**sue **pur**ely correct
  grammar.

put**ref**y (to rot): **Lef**t alone with no light or water, the plant began
  to put**ref**y. [See also "English Grammar and Pronunciation."]

py**k**nic (possessing a short, broad, and muscular body): Unlike
  the **yak**, a gorilla is py**k**nic.

Q

quan**ti**ty: It's a **pi**ty about the low quan**ti**ty.

quarant**ine** (to isolate, especially to protect others from
  contagious disease): We couldn't d**ine** with those under
  quarant**ine**.

questio**nn**aire: When the questio**nn**aire contained questions
  about my i**nn**er life, it provoked my **ire**.

qu**iet** (state of stillness or rest): Jul**iet** liked to enjoy her d**iet** in
  qu**iet**.

qu**ire** (set of 24 sheets of paper): **Qui**ckly get me a qu**ire** of paper.

qu**ite** (completely; positively): The dirty snow was not qu**ite**
  wh**ite**.

qui**zz**es: Bu**zz** passed all his qui**zz**es.

R

rac**coo**n: The rac**coo**n had chewed on my **acc**ount b**oo**k.

r**ail** (to complain): The carpenter would r**ail** against the use of
  any cheap n**ail**.

r**ale** (sound heard in labored breathing): When the doctor
  heard the m**ale** patient's breathing, the r**ale** was obvious.

rans**om**: The rans**om** was fr**om** someone unknown.

ra**pport** (harmonious relationship): We developed a good
  ra**pport** when you decided to su**pport** the air**port**.

rar**e**fy (to make thin, less dense, or more refined): To rar**e**fy is to make more rar**e**. [See also "English Grammar and Pronunciation."]

ras**p**berry: Give the man with the ras**p**y voice a ras**p**berry.

ration**a**le (basic reason or explanation for something): The ration**a**le for the s**a**le was declining business.

realistic**ally**: Realistic**ally**, **Sally** was your **ally**.

re**al**ize: We didn't re**al**ize you had missed a m**eal**.

re**ally**: Are you re**ally** brut**ally** frank?

rec**ede** (to depart or withdraw): After they b**ede**viled Jason, he chose to rec**ede** from his position.

rec**ei**pt (proof of purchase): The museum curator gave a rec**ei**pt for the fossilized **pt**erodactyl bones.

rec**eive**: You'll rec**eive** your package after you conc**eive** a plan to perc**eive** a bargain.

rec**ipe**: The rec**ipe** called for a **ripe** banana.

rec**og**nize: He can easily rec**og**nize a h**og**.

re**comm**end: The athlete boasted that he'll break a **reco**rd in the su**mm**er if you re**comm**end one.

recr**uit**: The recr**uit** exchanged his s**uit** for a uniform.

re**fer**: **Ref**er the **ref** to the rules.

refe**rr**ed: The minister assured his congregation that no one is refe**rr**ed to heaven in **err**or.

reg**ime** (ruling government): The reg**ime** of the government included a reg**ime**n of tough regulations.

re**hear**se: **Hear** me re**hear**se.

r**eign** (royal authority or rule): During his r**eign**, the sove**reign** would d**eign** to talk with commoners.

relev**a**nt: The comedian delivered a relev**a**nt r**a**nt.

rel**ie**f: Please **lie** down to get rel**ie**f.

relig**iou**s: Melvin gave an **IOU** as a relig**iou**s offering.

remini**scence** (recollection): The **scene** was ni**ce** because of remini**scence**.

rende**z**vous (place for meeting): We decided to use the **z**oo for our rende**z**vous.

re**now**n (fame): **Now** you have achieved re**now**n.

repent**a**nt (sorry): **Sant**a appreciated the repent**a**nt child.

rep**et**ition: You'll play the t**rumpet** better after rep**et**ition of practice.

rescind (cancel): We'll need to **resch**edule or **resc**ind the order.

resemblance: **Blanc**he was known for her resem**blanc**e to her mother.

reser**voir** (a place where water is collected): His **voi**ce **reso**nated at the reser**voir**.

resistance: **Lance** had developed resist**ance** to the germs.

response: **Se**ek my respon**se**.

restaurant: The rest**aura**nt had a pleasant **aura**.

rev**eille** (call to soldiers or campers to awaken, often sounded by a bugle): **Neil le**ft after he heard rev**eille**.

rever**ie** (daydream; condition of being lost in thought): When we called out Queen**ie**'s name, we disturbed her rever**ie**.

revue (light theatrical entertainment, especially of musical comedy acts): After seeing serious drama, we were overd**ue** for a rev**ue**.

rhapsody (musical composition): We were **hap**py with the **rhy**thm of the **rhap**sody.

rhetorical (pertaining to effective language): People who eat **rh**ubarb in **Rh**ode Island may also like **rh**etorical **rh**ymes of **rh**apsodic **rh**esus monkeys.

rhinocerous: A **rh**eumatoid **rh**inocerous can use **rh**etorical **rh**ythms to **rh**apsodize.

rhyme (set of words that sound alike): **H**enry loved **hym**ns and **rhym**es.

rhythm: **Rh**ythm **h**as **y**our **t**wo **h**ips **m**oving.

ridiculous: We decided to get **rid** of **rid**iculous clothes.

ro**le** (part in a play or movie): The actor played a ro**le** of someone on the d**ole**.

ro**ll** (to turn): Please don't r**oll** the d**oll**.

roo**mm**ate: The noisy roo**mm**ate was a bu**mm**er.

rough (course; difficult): The ride was t**ough**, r**ough**, and more than en**ough**.

rou**te** (course): He sc**out**ed for the best r**out**e.

S

saccharine (excessively sweet or sentimental): M**ac**'s **char**acter was a s**acchar**ine one.

sacrifice: **If** you move to a city with much **cri**me, you may have to sa**crif**ice some security.

sacrilegious (violating something sacred): The sac**rile**gious man faced ex**ile** when he began to **rile** people.

safety: If you want to make yourself **safe**, you'll need to think about **safe**ty.

salad: **Sal** got a good sal**ad**.

salve (medicinal, soothing ointment): We put s**alve** on her tender c**alve**s.

sandal (shoe): **Al** lost a sand**al**.

sandwich: Some **sand** in Mun**ich** got into my **sandwich**.

sapphire (precious blue stone): His girlfriend becomes **sapp**y around **sapp**hire.

satellite (orbiting object): Please **tell** us about Pluto's sa**tell**ite.

satisfaction: Is your satis**faction** a **fact**?

satisfactorily: Her l**ily** was watered satisfacto**rily**.

satisfied: He tr**ied** but was not satisf**ied**.

scaly (having scales): The shampoo helped Ray's **scaly** scalp.

scandal (embarrassing situation): **Randal** was involved in the sc**andal**.

scarcity: He received a **scar** in a **city** of **scar**city.

scary: We were w**ary** of seeing the sc**ary** movie.

scene (portion of film or play): It was a s**cary** s**cene**.

scent: Picking at the s**cab** caused an unpleasant s**cent**.

schedule: At **sch**ool the **rule** required following the **sch**ed**ule**.
   ▪ On his **sch**ed**ule**, he needed a Por**sche**, not a m**ule**.

scheme (plan): His **sch**eme was hatched in **sch**ool.

schist (mineral-laden rock): **Ch**uck recognized the s**chi**st as a metamorphic rock.

scholar (learned person): At s**ch**ool **Lar**s was a s**ch**o**lar**.

scissors: The Boy **Sc**out mi**ss**ed the **sciss**ors.

sculptor: The sculp**tor or** the instruc**tor** will meet with you.

sculpture: The sculp**ture** showed a ma**ture** style.

secede (to withdraw): His hair began to re**cede** before his state decided to se**cede** from the Union.

secretary: There is no **secret** unknown to the **secret**ary.

seize: At the height of our leisure, we seized neither foreign counterfeiters nor weird drugs.

semester: I took a seminar this semester.

senator: Senator Frist was a doctor before he became a senator.

sensible: In reading the Bible, Jimmy was the sensible sibling.

sentence: The sentence contained ten words.

separate: You'll find a rat and a rate in *separate*.

sergeant: The sergeant was stationed near the Bering Sea.

serial (story presented in separate parts): The serial contained a series of serious stories.

several: Al had several albums.

severe (harsh): There in Montana weather can be severe.

sheer (very thin; absolute; pure): Reese wore her sheer summer dress.

sheik (Arab leader): At eight, we met the sheik.

shepherd: Each shepherd had a herd of sheep.

sherbet: Her bet was for sherbet.

sheriff: We saw dandruff on the sheriff directing traffic.

shoo (exclamation meaning *Go away!*): We tried to shoo away the goose.

shoulder: You should tap him on the shoulder.

shriek (to utter a sharp, shrill sound): The cashier began to shriek during the robbery.

shrivel (to wither or shrink): The laurel tree began to shrivel.

siege: We didn't think that the alien would die in the siege.

similar: The military used similar tactics.

simile (comparison using *like* or *as*): We smile when we hear a simile.

  ▪ A simile is a smile with an eye (*I*).

simply: We should simply allow him to ply his trade.

simultaneous (happening at the same time): The tumult and explosion were simultaneous.

sincerely: Since you rely on me, I'll sincerely help you.

singe (to burn lightly): We noticed that the fire had begun to singe the hinge of the door.

site (location for a building, facility, or Internet page): We got a bite to eat at the site.

skiing: Skiing requires both eyes (*I*s).

snork**el** (device for breathing underwater): The child was in the mot**el** bathtub with a snork**el**.

sol**d**er (metal alloy): The **sold**er was already **sold**.

sol**di**er (military person): A sol**di**er must be willing to **die**.

s**ole** (bottom of foot or shoe): If your s**ole** contains more than one h**ole**, you might need new shoes.

s**ole** (kind of fish): He caught the s**ole** with a vi**ole**t p**ole**.

s**ole** (one and only): That part was the actor's s**ole** r**ole**.

sole**mn** (serious): He was the **sole man** to be **sole**mn.

so**me**r**saults**: Even **some** fa**ulty** so**me**r**saults** can thrill parents.

sometime (unspecified time): **Sometime** we'll realize that *sometime*, like *always*, is one word.

so**pho**more: The so**pho**more needed to **pho**ne home.

so**ur**ce: My enthusiasm began to **sour** when I learned about the **sour**ce of my friend's money.

sou**venir** (memento): In the **South**, s**ir**, I bought a sou**venir**.

spac**ious**: **I ow**e **us** a spac**ious** house.

spag**hetti**: **He** was in the at**ti**c with spag**hetti**.

specific**ally**: Specific**ally**, don't d**ally** at the r**ally**.

spe**ci**men (example or sample): We caught a **ci**cada as a spe**ci**men.

sp**ee**ch: The abduct**ee** had no fr**ee** sp**ee**ch.

spons**or**: The spons**or** of your doct**or or**dered more tests.

squ**eak**: The fr**eak** would sp**eak** with a squ**eak**.

squi**rr**el: The fu**rr**y animal was a squi**rr**el.

s**take** (pointed stick): Please don't **take** the s**take** from the ground.

stala**ct**ite (a deposit of calcium carbonate descending from the roof of a cave): Stala**ct**ites hang from the **c**eiling.

stala**g**mite (a deposit of calcium carbonate formed on the floor of a cave): A stala**g**mite is formed from the **g**round.

stam**pede**: I'll conc**ede** that a stam**pede** is no place for a **pede**strian.

sta**te**ment: The sta**te**ment was l**ate**.

station**ar**y (fixed in one place; standing): Something station**ar**y st**an**ds still.

station**er**y (paper and envelopes): The station**er**y is pap**er**.

st**eak** (slice of meat): St**eak** is m**eat**.

st**eal** (to take without permission): Don't st**eal** a m**eal**.

steel (metal alloy): The metal didn't have the feel of steel.

strait (narrow waterway): You need to wait for us to enter the strait.

strategy (plan): The poet's strategy was to write an elegy every week.

strength: English was her strength.

stubbornness: The tabby was known for her stubbornness.

subordinate (placed in a lower position): Nate resented his subordinate status.

subtle (not obvious): Sheila was subtle about her debt.

succeed: We'll succeed only if we proceed with caution and don't exceed the speed limit.

succession: The session ended after the succession of the officers.

succulent (juicy): Coco lent us a succulent fruit to use as a prop.

suede: Sue wore suede.

sufficient: One salient client is sufficient.

suffrage (right to vote): Women affronted men by demanding suffrage.

suing: His lawsuit involved suing over a shipment of fruit.

suite (group of connected rooms): Jake and his new suit entered the suite.

sundae (ice cream with syrup): How would you rate the sundae you just ate?

sundries (miscellaneous things): He tries to buy sundries.

superintendent (person in charge): The rent was sent to the superintendent.

supersede (to replace): These decrees supersede the old ones.

  ■ To supersede means to set aside.

superstitious: The institution housed some superstitious people.

supervisor: I received the order from the supervisor.

supplies: There lies the box of supplies.

suppress (subdue): Bill wasn't happy to suppress his feelings.

surgeon (doctor specializing in operations): Kurt knew the surgeon helped heal his hurt.

surprise: Burt didn't rise at the surprise.

surround: When I'm in a hurry, please don't surround me.

susceptible (open to some influence, stimulus, or agency): **S**cott used to believe that the **Bible** is susce**ptible** to more than one interpretation.

suspicious: We had no reasons to be suspi**cious** of our gra**cious** host.

sweat (perspiration): Both the h**eat** and his strenuous f**eat** made Ken sw**eat**.

sweet (opposite of sour): There was nothing sw**eet** about his f**eet**.

sword: It is hard to **sw**im with a **sw**ord.

syllable: We knew him b**y all** his sy**ll**ables.

symbol (something standing for something else): The fish is an **ol**d symb**ol**.

sympathy: We chose to sa**y** how we felt with a **sy**mpathy card.

synagogue (Jewish temple): **Y**ehudi didn't want to ar**gue** in the synago**gue**.

synonym (word with the same meaning as another): The expression *by the by* is a **sy**nonym of *incidentally*.

syphilis (a disease): We don't know **Y** (why) **Phil is** a person with sy**phil**is.

T

tail (rear of something): When the dog began to f**ail**, he left with his t**ail** between his legs.

tailor: The tai**lor** mended clothes for the sai**lor**.

taking: Some **kid** was ta**kid**ng my newspaper.

tale (story): D**ale** was a t**ale**nted teller of t**ale**s.

tambourine (musical instrument): He liked to play **our** tamb**our**ine.

tangible (capable of being touched; material): Some people want tang**ible** proof of miracles described in the **Bible**.

tariff (import tax): Even **riff**raff were required to pay the ta**riff**.

tassel: I never saw an **elf** wear a tass**el**.

tattoo: Pat, **too**, got a ta**ttoo**.

taupe (brownish gray color): The customer preferred t**aupe** to m**auve**.

tea (beverage): **E**ach had t**ea**.

technical: **Ch**arlotte was in a te**ch**nical field.

technique: You can rea**ch** your **que**st with the proper te**ch**ni**que**.

tee (holder for a golf ball): He placed the t**ee** near the tr**ee**.

televise: It was not w**ise** to telev**ise** the position of our troops.

temperamental (fickle; unpredictable in mood): **Ve**ra was tem**pera**mental.

temperature: The je**rk** was not m**ature** when he was running a temp**erature**.

temporary: The fast **tempo** of the **por**ter's work was only **tempor**ary.

tenant (person renting a dwelling): The **tenants** complained about the **ten ants**.

tendency (inclination): **Den**ny had a ten**den**cy to work in the gar**den**.

tentacle (arm-like appendage): **Ta**ra's t**en**t**a**cles were always reaching for **Ta**te's wallet.

terrible: Starting the fight was a t**err**ible **err**or.

testimonial (expression of appreciation): **Ji**m gave the coach a brief test**i**monial under the r**im**.

than (conjunction used in comparisons): Joyce's **han**ds are larger **than** yours.

their (possessive of *they*): **He ir**ked t**heir h**ei**rs**.

then (at that time): The word *then* tells you w**hen**.

theory: **Leo** likes his th**eo**ry.

there (at or in that place): **Sh**e**re** was **here**, not **there**.

therefore (consequently): He t**ore** the sheet and must, there**fore**, pay to replace it.

they're (contraction of *they are*): *Aid for use:* Can you meaningfully substitute "they are"? They're [They are] concerned about their health.

thief (one who steals): A th**ief** stole the p**ie**.

thoroughly (completely): The Norse god **Thor** was a thor**ough**ly **rough** character.

though (despite): He br**ough**t food, th**ough** he didn't eat.

threw (past tense of *throw*): We thr**ew** a f**ew** balls to L**ew**.

through (past): I **ough**t to drive th**rough** the **rough** neighborhood.

till (until): Please eat t**ill** you reach your f**ill**.

to (in the direction of): **Go to To**m's.

tobacco: **Tob**y **acco**sted John while the latter was smoking **tobacco**.

together: Were all of you **together** when it was time **to get her**?

tomatoes: I dropped toma**toes** and pota**toes** on the **toes** of her**oes**.

tomorrow: **Tom** will scu**rry tom**orrow.

tongue: The gl**ue** from the stamp got on his tong**ue**.

too (also): She **too**ted her horn for me **too**?

torpedoes: The her**oes** fired the torped**oes**.

tough (difficult; strong): I th**ough**t she was **tough** and r**ough** en**ough** to make it thr**ough** the competition.

tournament: The were f**our men** in the t**our**nament.

tow (to pull): The horse had to t**ow** the injured s**ow**.

toward (in the direction of): **Ward** Cleaver moved to**ward** Wally.

tragedy: Carolyn flew into a **rage** during the **tra**gedy.

transferred (moved): B**arry** was transf**err**ed in **err**or.

treacherous (traitorous): The p**reacher** was corrupt and t**reacher**ous.

trespass: Jean was **sassy** when she began to t**re**spass on the property.

    ■ All people who intentionally t**re**spass choose to t**ra**sgress the law.

tries: He t**ries** to cover his l**ies**.

trouble: **You** need to get **out** of trou**ble**.

troupe (group of actors or singers): Our tr**oupe** sang and never simply m**ou**thed lyrics.

truly (really; genuinely): It was tr**uly** a hot day in **July**.

Tucson: When spelling *Tucson* you must get *C* before *S*, as in the alphabet.

Tuesday: On **Tues**day you'll need to pay your d**ues**.

turkey: While you decided to mon**key** with your **key**, I prepared the tur**key**.

twelfth: Santa lost the twe**lfth elf**.

two (number after one): **Tw**ain began to **tw**ist and **tw**irl the **two tw**ins.

tying (binding): Pam was tr**ying** to avoid cr**ying** while t**ying** the dog.

tyranny: **Lynn** hated t**yra**nny.

U

unanimous (completely agreeing): **Nan, I'm** afraid the **ous**ter involved a u**nanimous** decision.

uncontrollable: The cartoon depicted a mischievous and uncon**troll**able **troll**.

underrate (to estimate too low): To und**err**ate your opponent is an **err**or.

undoubtedly (certainly): Undoub**ted**ly, I l**ed Ted** to b**ed**.

unforgettable: The man, himself un**forgettable**, began to **forget table**s.

university: The professor decided to **sit** on my univer**sit**y committee.

unnecessary (unneeded): A**nne**'s **cess**pool was u**nnecess**ary.

until: I won't eat un**til** we find some **til**apia fish.

usable (capable of being used): The **sable** was definitely u**sable**.

usage: When it comes to English u**sage**, H. W. Fowler was a **sage**.

useful: A cup**ful** will be use**ful**.

using: You can't **sing** without u**sing** your voice.

usually (most often): Usu**ally Sally** was my **ally**.

Utah: **Ah**, Ut**ah** is not the Sah**ah**a.

V

vaccine (substance taken to produce immunity to a disease): You need to **acc**ept the v**acc**ine with **acc**uracy.

vacuum: We need to va**cuu**m **cut**e Uma's carpet.

vale (valley): **Vale**rie, who lived in a **vale**, enjoyed looking at the mountains.

valuable (of value): Having d**ual** citizenship can be val**ua**ble.

vanilla: The French van**illa** ice cream made her **ill**.

various (different): Vince and Rob insist on upright stories. *(V**ar**ious)* var**ious**

vary (to change): **M**ary was w**ary** of opinions that v**ary**.

vegetable: You need to **get** a ve**get**able when you're **able**.

veil (cloth worn by women covering their heads and shoulders): **Ei**ght of the Iranian women wore v**ei**ls.

veneer (thin layer of material or facing; superficial quality or manner): The engin**eer** had only a ven**eer** of nontechnical knowledge.

ven**gea**nce (revenge): The dictator's desire for ven**gea**nce threw him out of **gea**r.

vete**ran**: The vete**ran ran** home to see a TV report on I**ran**.

vet**erin**arian (animal doctor): **Erin** took her dog to the vet**erin**arian.

vi**al** (small bottle): **Mia** carried a vi**al** of lotion in her purse.

vi**c**inity (proximity): **Vic** was not in this vi**c**inity.

vi**cious**: **V**ery **i**nsecure **c**ustomers **i**nsist **o**n **u**psetting **s**alespeople.

vi**ctim**: Don't let **Kim** or **Jim** become a vi**ctim**.

vi**gila**nt: We must be vi**gila**nt at the **gala**.

vi**lla**ge: The **lla**ma lived in the vi**lla**ge.

vi**llain** (evildoer): The vi**llain** took a **pill** on the tr**ain**.

vi**ole**nce: The p**ole** was used for vi**ole**nce.

vi**rtue**: **V**ery **i**ntelligent **r**oommates **t**rust **u**nderstanding **e**ngineers [or **e**arthlings].

vis**ible** (capable of being seen): The food was vis**ible** but not ed**ible**.

vi**sion**: **V**ery **i**nsightful **s**tudents **i**nsist **o**n **n**ovelty [or **n**etworking or **n**onconformity].

vita**min**: I thought the **min**t was a vita**min**.

vol**ume**: His neighbor began to f**ume** about the vol**ume** at the party.

W

w**ail** (to cry): The dog began to w**ail** when it stepped on a n**ail**.

w**ai**st (middle of the body): The m**ai**l carrier had a trim w**ai**st.

w**are** (product for sale): Where **are** your w**are**s?

w**arra**nt (authorization; justification): Once they saw the sheriff's w**arra**nt, the official began to **arra**y the prisoners.

w**arrior** (one engaged in warfare): **W**ar **a**nd **r**etaliation **r**eally **i**njure **o**rdinary **r**ustics.

w**aste** (to squander): Please don't w**aste** my p**aste**.

wea**lth**: **Wea**lth can buy a fancy m**ea**l but not necessarily good h**ea**lth.

wear (to have on the body): Don't **fear** to **wear** something over each **ear**.

weather (atmospheric conditions): Are **we at her** estate in this bad **weather**?

Wednesday (the day after Tuesday): **We do n**ot eat soup to**day**.

weigh (to determine the weight or importance of something): I decided to **weigh eigh**t **neigh**bors.

weird: At the **height** of our **leisure**, we **neither seized eigh**t **weird** for**eigne**rs nor forf**eite**d **eith**er prot**ein** shakes or fr**eigh**t.

welcome: We felt **welcome** at the hot**el**.

wharf (dock): We saw a **wharf** at the **har**bor.

whether (in case): Let me know **when** you know **whether** you'll attend my party.

whole (complete): The sow **h**ad the **whole** pen to herself.

wholly (completely): **Polly** was wh**olly** to blame.

whose (belonging to which person): Wh**ose rose** is my n**ose** smelling?

wintry (concerning winter): We wanted to **try** a win**try** blanket.

witch (woman with magical powers): **Mitch** was introduced to the w**itch**.

withdrawal: **Al** was giving up drugs and undergoing with-draw**al**.

woman: The **woman** liked the shade of the **oak**.

women: Matt liked to meet s**ome women**.

worthwhile (valuable): He decided to **work while** he listened to **worthwhile** conversation.

wrap (to enclose): Please use the bow **r**ight here when you **wrap** the gift after you **write** your name on the card.

wring (to squeeze): After I **wring** out the **wash**, I'll **wring** Walter's neck.

writing: **Tim** loved writing.

written: Terry had wr**itten** about my k**itten**.

X

xylophone (musical instrument): We saw e**xtra** parking at the **Y** for your **xylophone** concert.

Y

yacht: Did the author Bill Buckley ever listen to **Bach** on his **yach**t?

yeoman (petty officer): The right e**ye of** the **yeo**man was red.

yield: We must y**ie**ld the truth and not l**ie**.

yolk (yellow part of an egg): During Halloween your **fo**lks had **yo**lks on their windows.

Z

zenith (highest point): The **z**ookeeper was at the **z**enith of her career.

zinc: **C**arl needed zin**c** for his reproductive health.

ENGLISH SPELLING RULES

Although English spelling contains many irregularities and inconsistencies, the following rules can help you spell thousands of difficult words.

Double Consonants

- Double the last consonant before adding an ending to words with one syllable ending in both a single vowel and a single consonant.

  Examples: stop, stopped, stopping; fat, fatter, fattest
  Exceptions: words ending in *X*: box, boxing; mix, mixing

The Floss Rule

- One-syllable words ending in *F*, *L*, or *S* after a short vowel will usually end in a double consonant.

  Examples: sniff, snuff, hall, pass, dell

Drop the Final E

- Drop the E when the ending begins with a vowel (such as *-ing*, *-ed*, *-ous*, *-able*, *-y*).

- The E will fly
  Before you try
  To add a vowel ending.

  Examples: love, loving; prove, provably; nervous, nervous
  Exceptions: courageous, noticeable (*E* is needed to keep the *G* and *C* soft, sounding like *J* and *S*, respectively).

- Keep the final E when the suffix begins with a consonant (as in *-ment*, *-ful*, *-ly*).

  Examples: amuse, amusement; care, careful
  Exceptions: ninth, truly

Add *-ness* to a Word

- Add *-ness* without changing the root word unless the root word ends in *Y*.

  Examples: same, sameness; deaf, deafness
  Exceptions: happy, happiness; silly, silliness

Add *-ful* to a Word

- Add *-ful* (with one *L* only) when the suffix is used to mean "full of."

  Examples: cup, cupful; power, powerful
  Exceptions: none (How wonderful!)

I Before or After an *E*?

- *I* before *E*
  Except after *C*,
  Or in rhyming with *A*,
  As in *neighbor* or *weigh*.

Examples (*I* before *E*): brief, priest, chief

Examples (except after *C*): receive, deceive, ceiling

Examples (sounded as *A*): neighbor, reindeer, heinous

Exceptions:[98] Neither leisured foreign counterfeiter could seize either weird height without forfeiting protein.

Change a Final *Y* to an *I*

▪ Change the *Y* to an *I* when adding the endings *-ly*, *-ness*, or *-age* to a word ending in *Y*.

Examples: heavy, heaviness; happy, happily; carry, carriage; easy, easily

Exceptions: shy, shyly; sly, slyly

Add *-ly* to a Word

▪ Add *-ly* to the root word without changing anything.

Examples: open, openly; near, nearly; undoubted, undoubtedly

Exceptions: true, truly; whole, wholly

Form Compound Words

A compound word is formed by combining two individual words.

▪ Form a compound word by keeping both words whole.

Examples: gate+keeper=gatekeeper; ear+ring=earring; book+keeper=bookkeeper; room+mate=roommate

Exception: pastime

Add *-ing, -er,* or *-y* to Words Ending in C

▪ Add a *K* except when the ending begins with a consonant, such as *-ry*.

Examples: picnic, picnicking; traffic, trafficking; panic, panicky

Exception: mimicry

-ible vs. *-able*

- Look at the root. If the root is a complete word (is all there), the ending is usually *-able*. If the root isn't a complete word, the ending is *-ible*.

   Examples: agree + able = agreeable;   teach + able = teach-able
   Examples: poss + ible = possible; vis + ible = visible

Plurals of Words Ending in *O*

- Add *S* to a word that ends in an *O* preceded by a vowel.
- Add *ES* to a word that ends in an *O* preceded by a consonant.
- Add *S* to music terms ending in *O*.

   Examples: radio, radios; rodeo, rodeos
   Examples: potato, potatoes; hero, heroes
   Qualified exceptions: mosquito, mosquitoes (preferred) or mosquitos (acceptable); tornado, tornados (preferred) or tornadoes (acceptable)
   Examples: solo, solos; piano, pianos

Possessives of Pronouns: *It, Her,* and *Their*

- Do not use an apostrophe.

   Examples: The dog chewed its bone. The car is hers. The tree is theirs.

Negative Prefixes: *mis-, un-, in-, dis-, ir-,* and *il-*

- Keep the root word unchanged whenever you add a prefix to turn a word into its opposite.

   Examples: possible, impossible; necessary, unnecessary; spell, misspell; legal, illegal; mature, immature; religious, irreligious

Common Silent *G* Words[99]

▪ The **gnar**led **gnome gnash**ed his teeth as he **gnaw**ed a **gnat**.

Common Silent *H* Words[100]

▪ A **rheumatic rhinoceros** practices **rhetorical rhymes** while eating **rhododendrons** and **rhubarb** in **Rhode** Island.

What to Capitalize

▪ **D**inner **MINTS**

Days of the week	Names of people, places, and
Months of the year	things
I (pronoun)	Titles (books, plays, movies)
	Start of a sentence

TIME AND CALENDARS

- -

The 12 Months

▪ **J**an **f**ound **M**ark **a**nd **M**ay **j**eering **j**oylessly **at S**arah **o**utside **N**athan's **D**eli.

January	July
February	August
March	September
April	October
May	November
June	December

Months: July to December (in Order)

- JASON D

July	October
August	November
September	December

Number of Days per Month

- Thirty days hath September,
  April, June, and November,
  February eight-and-twenty all alone
  And all the rest have thirty-one,
  Unless that Leap Year doth combine
  And give to February twenty-nine.

- Thirty days hath November,
  April, June, and September,
  February hath twenty-eight alone,
  And all the rest have thirty-one.

- Fourth, eleventh, ninth, and sixth,
  Thirty days to affix;
  Every other thirty-one,
  Except the second month alone.

Easter

- No need for confusion if we but recall
  That Easter on the first Sunday after the full moon
  Following the vernal equinox doth fall.

Daylight Savings Time: Resetting Clocks

- Spring forward; fall back.

A Year's Calendar in Your Head

To figure out on which day of the week a particular date falls, you need only memorize one 12-digit number. Here's how it works. Each digit represents the date of the first Sunday in each month in order. As an example, I'll use 2007. What are the dates of the first Sundays in each month for 2007? For January 2007, the first Sunday falls on the 7th, in February it falls on the 4th, and in March it also falls on the 4th. Thus the first three digits of our 12-digit mnemonic is 744. Here are all the first Sundays for 2007:

MONTH	DATE OF FIRST SUNDAY
January	7
February	4
March	4
April	1
May	6
June	3
July	1
August	5
September	2
October	7
November	4
December	2

Dividing the mnemonic into 3-digit chunks, the 12-digit number is 744-163-152-742. Using that number and some simple arithmetic, we can figure out the day on which any date in 2007 falls without having to look at a calendar.

Note: For example, what day of the week is July 4, 2007? The 7th month is represented by the 7th digit of our 12-digit mnemonic: 1. That fact means that July 1, 2007, is a Sunday. It follows that July 4, 2007, must be a Wednesday. As another example, what day of the week is September 16, 2007? Since September is the 9th month, we need the 9th digit of our 12-digit number, which is 2. Because September 2, 2007, falls on a Sunday, September 16, exactly two weeks later, must also be a Sunday.

Calendar Mnemonic for 2008

- 632-641-637-527

Note: As an example, on what day of the week is July 4, 2008? The 7th digit is 6, meaning that the first Sunday in July 2008 is on July 6. It follows that July 4 must be on Friday (the first one in July).

First of Each Month: Day of the Week[101]

For this device, if you know the day on which January 1 falls in any year, you can determine the day on which the first of any other month falls in that year.

- **At D**over **d**welt **G**eorge **B**rown, **E**squire, **g**ood **C**hristopher **F**inch, **a**nd **D**avid **F**ryer.

Note: As an example, let's take 2007. In 2007, January 1 fell on a Monday, represented by the first word in the mnemonic. Because the first day of July is in the 7th month, July 1 is represented by the 7th word, *good*, which begins with G. The letter G is six letters after A in the alphabet; counting six days after Monday (January 1, 2007), we get Sunday. Therefore, July 1, 2007, is a Sunday. In leap years, you need to add one extra day to the calculations for all months after February.

Adjust for the International Dateline

- When it's Sunday in San Francisco, it's Monday in Manilla.

WEATHER

Layers of the Atmosphere[102]

- Layers of the atmosphere,
  Atmosphere, atmosphere,
  Layers of the atmosphere,
  The air surrounding earth.

  The troposphere is twelve miles high.
  Dust and clouds are floating by.
  Gas and vapor are in supply
  In the troposphere.

  The stratosphere is thirty miles high.
  Icy winds are blowing by.
  The air is very clear and dry
  In the stratosphere.

  The mesosphere is fifty miles high.
  Temperatures get cold, no lie!
  Minus one hundred degrees Fahrenheit
  In the mesosphere.

  The exosphere is three hundred ten miles high.
  Separating earth and space, oh my!
  Satellites are passing by
  In the exosphere.

  The thermosphere is four hundred miles high.
  Electrical ions are in supply.
  Radio waves and beams bounce by
  In the thermosphere.

Note: Sing to the tune of "Mary Had a Little Lamb."

Types of Clouds[103]

- **[Chorus]**
  The sky has many types of clouds,
  Types of clouds, types of clouds.
  The sky has many types of clouds,
  Classified by height.

  Stratus clouds are low and gray,
  Sheetlike clouds producing rain.
  Stratocumulus are much the same,
  Low, dark, heavy clouds.

  Cumulus clouds are also low,
  White and piled up, you know.
  Cumulonimbus are very low.
  They bring heavy showers.
  [Chorus]
  Altostratus are grayish sheets,
  Up six thousand to twenty thousand feet.
  Altocumulus look so neat,
  Fleecy clouds in blue sky.

  Cirrus clouds are way up high,
  Twenty thousand to forty thousand feet in the sky.
  Wispy clouds with crystals of ice,
  Those are cirrus clouds.

  Cirrostratus are just as high,
  Milky, thin clouds in the sky.
  Cirrocumulus are thin cloud lines
  With ripples on their edges.
  [Chorus]

  Note: Sing to the tune of "The Wheels on the Bus."

Weather Predictions

- The South wind brings wet weather;
  The North wind wet and cold together;
  The West wind brings us rain;
  The East wind blows it back again.

- When clouds appear like rocks and towers,
  The earth's refreshed by frequent showers.

- If the First of July be rainy weather,
  It will rain, more or less, for four weeks together.

- If there be a rainbow in the eve,
  It will rain and leave.
  But if there be a rainbow in the morrow,
  It will neither lend nor borrow.

- Ring around the moon:
  It'll rain soon.

- Red sky in the morning,
  Sailors, take warning.
  Red sky at night,
  Sailors' delight.

- The evening red, and the morning gray,
  Are the tokens of a bonny day.

- Onion skin very thin:
  Mild winter coming in.
  Onion skin thick and tough:
  Coming winter cold and rough.

Celsius: Relative Temperature

- 5, 10, and 21
  winter, spring, and summer fun.

ZODIAC

The 12 Signs in Order[104]

- Our vernal signs the **Ram** begins, then comes the **Bull**, in May the **Twins**; the **Crab** in June, next **Leo** shines, and **Virgo** ends the northern signs. The **Balance** brings autumnal fruits, the **Scorpion** stings, the **Archer** shoots; December's **Goat** brings wintry blast; **Aquarius** rain, the **Fish** comes last.
- As the great cook likes very little salt, she compensates adding pepper.

Aries	Libra
Taurus	Scorpio
Gemini	Sagittarius
Cancer	Capricorn
Leo	Aquarius
Virgo	Pisces

ZOOLOGY

----

6 Groups of Purebred Dogs

- Nothing hounds workers sporting terrific toupees.

nonsporting   sporting
hound   terrier
working   toy

Insect's Leg: Parts

- Cockroaches travel for the tasty children.

coxa   tibia
trochanter   tarsus
femur   claw

Frogs: Arteries Branching off Aorta (in Order)

- Little men in short black mackintoshes

lingual   subclavian
mandibular   brachial
innominate   musculocutaneous

Bears: Cubs at Birth

- Bear bear bare bears.

Newborn bears are hairless.

Coral Snake vs. King Snake

- Red and yellow, kill a fellow.
  Red and black, friend of Jack.

  Note: Coral snakes are venomous, and king snakes are not.

Alligators vs. Crocodiles

- Now, a crocodile is hardly a runt,
  But the alligator's snout is shorter and more blunt.
  These two reptiles are of the same group—
  If you meet them both at once, then you're the soup.

NOTES

1. Heinlein, *Have Space Suit—Will Travel*, 109.
2. Rossetti, *The Poetical Works of Christina Georgina Rossetti*, 442.
3. Jernigan, "Remembering the Chicago Black Sox," *The National Pastime*, 33: 94.
4. Benne, *Waspleg and Other Mnemonics: Easy Ways to Remember Hard Things*, 133.
5. Benne, 133.
6. Benne, 133.
7. Ferraro, *Remembrance of Things Fast*, 97.
8. Ferraro, 96. The *S* in Ferraro's "Go Corgis" has been omitted.
9. Ferraro, 101.
10. Benne, 43.
11. Benne, 43.
12. From "Periodic Table Mnemonics." Note that many of these devices conjure mental pictures, making them all the more useful. In fact, the website from which they are taken includes pictures. The mnemonics I modified contain brackets.
13. Gibson and Guastaferro, *How to Remember Everything, Grades 6–8*, 223.
14. Ferraro, 92.
15. *A Dictionary of Mnemonics*, 22.
16. Goldish, *Memory-Boosting Mnemonic Songs for Content Area Learning*, 23.
17. Benne, 109.
18. Benne, 109.
19. Benne, 135.
20. Benne, 135.
21. Benne, 138.
22. Goldish, 88.
23. Goldish, 61.
24. Benne, 74.
25. Slung, *The Absent-Minded Professor's Memory Book*, 19.
26. Slung, 19.
27. Ferraro, 30.
28. Benne, 71.
29. Benne, 71.
30. Benne, 73.
31. Benne, 75.
32. Adapted from Benne, 150, containing Benne's mnemonic for seven countries (the G7); I've adapted the mnemonic to include Russia.
33. Benne, 110.
34. Benne, 111.
35. Benne, 110–111.
36. Slung, 10–11.
37. Slung, 11.

38. Slung, 11.

39. Devices with an asterisk (*) are from Cody, *Teaching Out of the Box*, and those without an asterisk are mine.

40. Benne, 121–122.

41. Benne, 18.

42. Slung, 3.

43. Goldish, 57.

44. Goldish, 56.

45. Slung, 14.

46. Slung, 10.

47. Slung, 16.

48. Benne, 137.

49. Benne, 111.

50. Kennedy, *The Shorter Latin Primer*, 109.

51. *A Dictionary of Mnemonics*, 43.

52. *A Dictionary of Mnemonics*, 44.

53. Benne, 47

54. Gibson and Guastaferro, 152.

55. Gibson and Guastaferro, 164.

56. Benne, 45.

57. Gibson and Guastaferro, 171.

58. Gibson and Guastaferro, 172.

59. Gibson and Guastaferro, 177.

60. Gibson and Guastaferro, 178.

61. Kahn and Meltzer, *How to Remember Everything, Grades 9–12*, 173.

62. Slung, 49.

63. Ferraro, 64. First created for a 1951 mnemonic contest held by Lloyds Bank International under the direction of Lord Balfour of Burleigh and printed in a company publication.

64. Goldish, 78.

65. Goldish, 76.

66. Goldish, 77.

67. Kahn and Meltzer, 195.

68. Benne, 65.

69. Benne, 129.

70. Benne, 130.

71. The first set of Morse Code mnemonics is available from numerous sources, including *A Dictionary of Mnemonics*, 54–55. Note that the usual *zoological* was changed to *zoologic* because four syllables are needed, not five. The second set of mnemonics is from Hale-Evans, *Mind Performance Hacks*, 208–209.

72. Benne, 100–101.

73. Goldish, 43.

74. Goldish, 44.

75. "Boating Definitions and Mnemonics" from Geoff Kuenning. The nautical advice on this website is intended to embody practical guidelines for safety and etiquette rather than official law.

76. Robinson, *Mnemonics & More for Psychiatry*, 91.

77. Robinson, 114.
78. Robinson, 118.
79. Robinson, 120.
80. Robinson, 93.
81. Robinson, 147.
82. Robinson, 122.
83. Robinson, 64.
84. Robinson, 83.
85. Robinson, 124.
86. Robinson, 126.
87. Robinson, 77.
88. Robinson, 128.
89. Robinson, 71.
90. Robinson, 73.
91. Robinson, 81.
92. Benne, 65.
93. Benne, 90.
94. Slung, 25.
95. Benne, 17.
96. Benne, 92.
97. Most of the words, pronunciations, and definitions are from Sarris, *Comic Mnemonics*. I created the mnemonics for *aprender, beber, comenzar, comprender, construir, contestar, creer, fumar, mirar, terminar,* and *vender.*
98. Suid, *Demonic Mnemonics*, 58.
99. Suid, 69
100. Suid, 121.
101. *A Dictionary of Mnemonics*, 52.
102. Goldish, 92.
103. Goldish, 90.
104. The first device is from Brewer, *Dictionary of Phrase and Fable*, 1175. The second device is from Benne, 34–35.

BIBLIOGRAPHY

PRINT SOURCES

Arden, John B. *Improving Your Memory for Dummies.* Hoboken, N.J.: Wiley, 2002.

Atkinson, R. C. "Mnemotechnics in Second-Language Learning." *American Psychologist* 30 (1975), 821–828.

Benne, Bart. *Waspleg and Other Mnemonics: Easy Ways to Remember Hard Things.* Dallas: Taylor, 1988.

Bloomfield, Robert L., and E. Ted Chandler, *Mnemonics, Rhetoric and Poetics for Medics.* Winston-Salem, N.C.: Harbinger Press, 1982.

Bloomfield, Robert L., and Carolyn F. Pedley, *Mnemonics, Rhetoric and Poetics for Medics.* Vol. 2. Winston-Salem, N.C.: Harbinger Press, 1984.

Brett, Simon, Ed. *The Faber Book of Useful Verse.* London: Faber & Faber, 1981.

Brewer, E. Cobham. *Dictionary of Phrase and Fable.* Ed. Ivor H. Evans. New York: Harper & Row, 1970.

Buzan, Tony. *The Brain User's Guide.* New York: Dutton, 1983.

Buzan, Tony. *Make the Most of Your Mind.* New York: Fireside, 1988.

Buzan, Tony. *The Mind Map Book.* New York: Plume, 1996.

Buzan, Tony. *Use Both Sides of Your Brain.* New York: Dutton, 1974.

Buzan, Tony. *Use Your Perfect Memory.* New York: Penguin, 1992.

Cermak, Laird S. *Improving Your Memory.* New York: Norton, 1984.

Chafetz, Michael. *Smart for Life: How to Improve Your Brain Power at Any Age.* New York: Penguin, 1992.

Clifford, M. M. "Thoughts on a Theory of Constructive Failure." *Educational Psychologist* 19 (1984): 108–120.

Cody, Stan. *Teaching Out of the Box.* Laguna Hills, Calif.: Stan Cody Publishing, 2006.

Crook, Thomas. *The Memory Cure.* New York: Pocket, 1998.

A Dictionary of Mnemonics. London: Eyre Methuen, 1972.

Ebbesmeyer, Joan. *Teaching Global Literacy Using Mnemonics.* Westport, Conn.: Teacher Ideas, 2006.

Ehri, L. C., N. D. Deffner, and L. S. Wilce. "Pictorial Mnemonics for Phonics." *Journal of Educational Psychology* 76 (1984): 880–893.

Felberbaum, Frank, and Rachel Kranz. *The Business of Memory.* New York: Rodale, 2005.

Ferraro, Susan. *Remembrance of Things Fast.* New York: Dell, 1990.

Fotuhi, Majid. *The Memory Cure.* New York: McGraw-Hill, 2003.

Furst, Bruno. *Stop Forgetting.* Garden City, N.Y.: Garden City Books, 1948.

Gibson, Ellen, and Nick Guastaferro. *How to Remember Everything, Grades 6–8.* New York: Random House, 2006.

Goldish, Meish. *Memory-Boosting Mnemonic Songs for Content Area Learning.* New York: Scholastic, 2006.

Goldman, Robert, Ronald Klatz, and Lisa Berger. *Brain Fitness.* New York: Doubleday, 1999.

Gordon, Barry, and Lisa Berger. *Intelligent Memory: Improve the Memory That Makes You Smarter.* New York: Viking, 2003.

Halacy, Don. *How to Improve Your Memory.* New York: Franklin Walts, 1977.

Hale-Evans, Ron. *Mind Performance Hacks: Tips & Tools for Overclocking Your Brain.* Sebastopol, Calif.: O'Reilly Media, 2006.

Hancock, Jonathan. *Maximise Your Memory.* St. Leonards, Australia: Allen & Unwin, 2000.1

Heinlein, Robert. *Have Space Suit—Will Travel.* New York: Ballantine, 2003.

Herold, Mort. *You'll Never Forget a Name Again!* Chicago: Contemporary, 1992.

Herrmann, D. J., and R. Chaffin. *Memory in Historical Perspective: The Literature before Ebbinghaus.* New York: Springer-Verlag, 1988.

Higbee, Kenneth L. *Your Memory—How It Works and How to Improve It.* Englewood Cliffs, N.J.: Prentice Hall, 1977.

Jernigan, Robert. "Remembering the Chicago Black Sox." *The National Pastime: A Review of Baseball History.* Society for American Baseball Research, 32 (2002): 94.

Kahn, Russell, and Tom Meltzer. *How to Remember Everything, Grades 9–12.* New York: Random House, 2006.

Kail, Robert. *The Development of Memory in Children.* New York: Freeman, 1989.

Kawashima, Ryuta. *Train Your Brain: 60 Days to a Better Brain.* Teaneck, N.J.: Kumon Publishing, 2005.

Kennedy, Benjamin Hall. *The Shorter Latin Primer*. London: Longmans, Green, 1962.

Khan, Khalid. *Mnemonics for Medical Students*. London: Hodder Arnold, 2003.

Lapp, Danielle C. *Maximizing Your Memory Power*. New York: Barron's Educational Series, 1992.

Levin, J. R., B. J. Dretzke, C. B. McCormick, T. E. Scruggs, J. E. McGivern, and M. A. Mastropieri. "Learning via Mnemonic Pictures: Analysis of the Presidential Process." *Educational Communication and Technology Journal* 3 (1983): 547–550.

Levin, J. R., C. R. Morrison, J. E. McGivern, M. A. Mastropieri, and T. E. Scruggs. "Mnemonic Facilitation of Text-Embedded Science Facts." *American Educational Research Journal* 23 (1986): 489–506.

Leviton, Richard. *Brain Builders*. Paramus, N.J.: Prentice Hall, 1995.

Lewis, David, and James Green. *Thinking Better*. New York: Rawson, Wade, 1982.

Liddon, Jo, and Huw Williams. *Memory Booster Workout*. San Diego, Calif.: Thunder Bay, 2003.

Lombard, Jay, and C. Germano. *The Brain Wellness Plan*. New York: Kensington Books, 1997.

Lorayne, Harry. *How to Develop a Super-Power Memory*. New York: Frederick Fell, 1957.

Lorayne, Harry. *Official Know-It-All Guide to Secrets of Mind Power*. Hollywood, Fla.: Frederick Fell, 2006.

Lorayne, Harry. *Super Memory Super Student*. New York: Little, Brown, 1990.

Lorayne, Harry, and Jerry Lucas. *The Memory Book*. New York: Stein & Day, 1974.

Luria, A. R. *The Mind of a Mnemonist*. Cambridge, Mass.: Harvard University Press, 1968.

Markowitz, Karen, and Eric Jensen. *The Great Memory Book*. San Diego, Calif: The Brain Store, 1999.

Marlowe, E. S. *Medico Mnemonica*. Los Angeles: Practice Management Information, 1997.

Mason, Douglas, and Michael Lee Kohn. *The Memory Workbook*. Oakland, Calif.: New Harbinger, 2001.

Mastropieri, M. A. "Using the Keyword Method." *Teaching Exceptional Children* 20, no. 2 (1988): 4–8.

Mastropieri, M. A., K. Emerick, and T. E. Scruggs. "Mnemonic Instruction of Science Concepts." *Behavioral Disorders* 14 (1988): 48–56.

Mastropieri, M. A., and T. E. Scruggs. "Mnemonic Social Studies Instruction: Classroom Applications." *Remedial and Special Education* 10, no. 3 (1989): 40–46.

Mastropieri, Margo A., and Thomas E. Scruggs. *Teaching Students Ways to Remember: Strategies for Learning Mnemonically.* Cambridge, Mass.: Brookline, 1991.

Mastropieri, M. A., T. E. Scruggs, and J. R. Levin. "Pictorial Mnemonic Strategies for Special Education." *Journal of Special Education Technology* 6 (1983): 24–33.

Mastropieri, M. A., T. E. Scruggs, and J. R. Levin. "Research in Progress: Mnemonic Strategies for Handicapped and Gifted Learners." *Exceptional Children* 50 (1984): 559.

Mastropieri, M. A., T. E. Scruggs, J. R. Levin, J. Gaffney, and B. McLoone. "Mnemonic Vocabulary Instruction for Learning Disabled Students." *Learning Disability Quarterly* 8 (1985): 57–63.

Michaud, Ellen, and Russell Wild. *Boost Your Brain Power.* Emmaus, Pa.: Rodale, 1991.

O'Brien, Dominic. *The Amazing Memory Kit: Everything You Need to Improve Your Memory!* San Diego, Calif.: Thunder Bay, 2005.

O'Brien, Dominic. *How to Develop a Brilliant Memory Week by Week.* London: Duncan Baird, 2005.

O'Brien, Dominic. *How to Pass Exams.* London: Duncan Baird, 2003.

O'Brien, Dominic. *Never Forget a Name or Face.* New York: Chronicle, 2002.

Paul, Kevin. *Study Smarter, Not Harder.* Bellingham, Wash.: Self-Counsel Press, 1996.

Pressley, M., and J. R. Levin, Eds. *Cognitive Strategy Training: Educational Applications and Theoretical Foundations.* New York: Springer-Verlag, 1983.

Pressley, M., J. R. Levin, and H. D. Delaney. "The Mnemonic Keyword Method." *Review of Educational Research* 52 (1982): 61–91.

Pressley, M., J. Samuel, M. M. Hershey, S. L. Bishop, and D. Dickinson. "Use of a Mnemonic Technique to Teach Young Children Foreign Language Vocabulary." *Contemporary Educational Psychology* 6 (1981): 110–116.

Robinson, David J., M.D. *Mnemonics & More for Psychiatry.* Port Huron, Mich.: Rapid Psychler, 2001.

Rossetti, Christina Georgina. *The Poetical Works of Christina Georgina Rossetti.* Ed. William Michael Rossetti. New York: Macmillan, 1979.

Rupp, Rebecca. *Committed to Memory.* New York: Crown, 1998.

Sandstrom, Robert. *The Ultimate Memory Book.* Granada Hills, Calif.: Stepping Stone, 1990.

Sarris, Jim. *Comic Mnemonics: A Fun, Easy Way to Remember Spanish Verbs.* Tarrytown, N.Y.: Alacan, 2004.

Scruggs, T. E., and M. A. Mastropieri. "Acquisition and Transfer of Mnemonic Strategies by Gifted and Non-Gifted Students." *Journal of Special Education* 22 (1988): 153–166.

Scruggs, T. E., and M. A. Mastropieri. "Spontaneous Verbal Elaboration in Gifted and Non-Gifted Youths." *Journal for the Education of the Gifted* 9 (1985): 1–10.

Scruggs, T. E., M. A. Mastropieri, C. Jorgensen, and J. A. Monson. "Effective Mnemonic Strategies for Gifted Learners." *Journal for the Education of the Gifted* 9 (1986): 105–121.

Seamon, J. G. *Human Memory.* New York: Oxford University Press, 1980.

Slung, Michele. *The Absent-Minded Professor's Memory Book.* New York: Ballantine, 1985.

Small, Gary. *The Memory Bible.* New York: Hyperion, 2002.

Small, Gary. *The Memory Prescription.* New York: Hyperion, 2004.

Sternberg, Robert J. *Intelligence Applied: Understanding and Increasing Your Intellectual Skills.* New York: Harcourt Brace Jovanovich, 1986.

Suid, Murray. *Demonic Mnemonics: 800 Spelling Tricks for 800 Tricky Words.* New York: Laurel, 1981.

Turkington, Carol. *12 Steps to a Better Memory.* New York: Macmillan, 1996.

Young, Morris N., and Walter B. Gibson. *How to Develop an Exceptional Memory.* North Hollywood, Calif.: Wilshire, 1970.

ONLINE SOURCES

Amanda's Mnemonics Page
www.netnaut.com/mnemonics.html
A widely linked site from Amanda Hargis. It contains mnemonics for several disciplines.

Boating Definitions and Mnemonics
http://ficus-www.cs.ucla.edu/ficus-members/geoff/mnemonics.html

An excellent site for boating mnemonics from computer scientist Geoff Kuenning.

Chatboard Poll: "What's Your Favorite Mnemonic?"
http://teachers.net/gazette/AUG00/poll.html
An article from *The Teachers.net Gazette* in which teachers contribute their favorite mnemonics for several disciplines.

Education World Professional Development Center: Teaching with Mnemonics
www.education-world.com/a_curr/profdev/profdev117.shtml
The site contains an article explaining how teachers can incorporate mnemonics into their teaching (" 'You Must Remember This' . . . Teaching with Mnemonics").

English Mnemonics-Wikiquote
http://en.wikiquote.org/wiki/English_mnemonics
Site containing popular mnemonics for several disciplines. Of particular note is the page for chemistry mnemonics.

EUdesign-Portfolio Index·
www.eudesign.com/mnems/_mnframe.htm
An ingenious site from Peter Hobbs containing mnemonics for several disciplines and extending more than 120 pages.

Kid Tips For Easy Learning
www.betterendings.org/homeschool/fun/mnemonic.htm
Site containing mnemonics for several disciplines.

Medical Mnemonics.com
www.medicalmnemonics.com
An impressively large site for medical mnemonics, including anatomy and physiology.

Periodic Table Mnemonics
www.aps.edu/aps/eisenhower/brugge/Periodic05.html
Site with chemical symbols depicted by words and pictures from Mr. Brügge's eighth-grade science students at Eisenhower Middle School, part of the Albuquerque public school system.

PERMISSIONS

ABOUT THE AUTHOR

Rod L. Evans, Ph.D., is a philosophy professor who has won two awards for outstanding teaching and who has written, co-written, or coedited fourteen books, including *Matching Wits with the Million-Dollar Mind*—a trivia book cowritten with John Carpenter, the first million-dollar winner on TV's *Who Wants to Be a Millionaire*— and *The Gilded Tongue: Overly Eloquent Words for Everyday Things*, a dictionary of unusual words.